PARENTING FOR £1

And Other Baby Budget Hacks

MARK & ROXANNE HOYLE

BANTAM PRESS

LONDON · TORONTO · SYDNEY · AUCKLAND · JOHANNESBURG

TRANSWORLD PUBLISHERS
61–63 Uxbridge Road, London W5 5SA
www.penguin.co.uk

Transworld is part of the Penguin Random House group of companies
whose addresses can be found at global.penguinrandomhouse.com

First published in Great Britain in 2018 by Bantam Press
an imprint of Transworld Publishers

Hack photographs and photos on pages 7 and 8 © Ladbaby
Additional images © Shutterstock

A CIP catalogue record for this book
is available from the British Library.

ISBN 9781787630161

Typeset in Helvetica Neue 11/16pt by Envy Design Ltd
Printed and bound in Italy by Printer Trento s.r.l.

Penguin Random House is committed to a sustainable
future for our business, our readers and our planet. This book
is made from Forest Stewardship Council® certified paper.

3 5 7 9 10 8 6 4 2

In loving memory of our social life and sanity.
Sadly lost at 3.30 a.m. on 1 April 2016 and at 10.55 a.m. on 29 May 2018.

CONTENTS

INTRODUCTION

For anyone who's ever stood in the baby section of a department store and thought, WTF, how on earth are they charging £200 for a miniature wicker basket for my baby to sleep in? – this book is for you!

The hardest thing about being a parent, other than the years spent changing nappies, the countless sleepless nights, accidentally bleaching all your favourite shirts with sterilizing solution and waving goodbye to your social life, is the eighteen-plus years of financial battering your bank account takes. Ordinarily, if someone were to come along and empty your account by buying themselves a new bed, a summer wardrobe, a year's worth of underwear, and an overly luxurious little chair to be pushed around in everywhere they go, you'd be calling the police and proclaiming daylight robbery. However, because you're somehow hardwired to love and support children who share half of your DNA you're willing to sacrifice almost anything to give them the very best in life … even if it means you yourself have to go without. For example, as I sit here writing this, I'm wearing a pair of jeans with a golf-ball-sized hole in the gusset, offering me something of a breeze around my crown jewels. Maybe that should be my first hack: Gusset Air-con? Maybe not …

Without question we'd all like to give our kids the very best. The only problem is … the baby industry knows this and is ready to take advantage at every turn! Like any opportunist, it preys on the weak and the vulnerable: NEW PARENTS! It knows that because we are feeling the peer pressure of other judgemental parents, experiencing the unexpected fright that parental responsibility of a miniature human brings, and dealing with the blind panic that we might now have to start acting like adults, we will spend almost anything for peace of mind – and to conquer parenthood once and for all.

Rox and I want *Parenting for £1* to help guide you through the early years of parenthood with a smile on your face and money in your pocket. It's not about being tight, it's about helping you to avoid some of Babyland's biggest expenses so that you can enjoy what parenthood is really all about … reliving your youth and raising happy kids!

Hold on to your wallets …

DISCLAIMER

WHILST ROX AND I HAVE PERSONALLY TRIED, TESTED AND LIVED THROUGH EVERY SINGLE HACK IN THIS BOOK OURSELVES, DO USE YOUR COMMON SENSE IF YOU'RE PLANNING TO RECREATE ANY! OBVIOUSLY THEY'RE ALL HOME-MADE AND HAVE BEEN THROUGH NO OFFICIAL SAFETY TESTING SO NEITHER MYSELF NOR ROX CAN BE HELD RESPONSIBLE FOR YOU LOSING A THUMB TRYING TO CUT YOUR KITCHEN DOOR IN HALF, FOR EXAMPLE, OR INDEED FOR ANYTHING ELSE. IT GOES WITHOUT SAYING, BUT PLEASE ONLY DO THINGS WITH YOUR FAMILY YOU FEEL TOTALLY COMFORTABLE WITH AND NEVER LEAVE A CHILD UNATTENDED. THAT'S GENERAL LIFE ADVICE BUT ALSO WORKS HERE TOO! BRILLIANT, NOW THAT'S OUT OF THE WAY AND I'M NOT WORRIED ABOUT BEING SUED OVER YOUR THUMB, LET'S CRACK ON.

THE LADBABY FAMILY

Don't ever let anyone tell you that nothing good comes from sambuca shots at 1 a.m. in a tiny basement bar in central London on a school night … because that's exactly how Rox and I met. In fact, 'Sambuca?' was the first thing I ever said to Rox, as I offered her a drink at the bar. I know, I know, offering a pretty girl a sambuca isn't exactly a textbook chat-up line (especially when you later find out she detests it!), but it worked like a charm and the rest is history … mainly because Rox insisted I add her as a friend on Facebook that very night because she thought … Er, I don't know what she thought. That I would vanish into the night never to be seen again, perhaps? How wrong she was.

After about a year of dating, we decided to move in together. We pooled our money and rented a studio flat on the outskirts of London. Yep, that's the joy of living in London: two wages and that's all you can afford. Anyway, appearances can be deceptive, and I still state to this day that it was the best place I've ever lived! Not only was it above a pub where the kitchen staff would give me free burgers out the back by the bins, but the room was so small I could open the fridge and start breakfast on the hob without even getting out of bed! It was incredible. To some people it might sound horrendous, but until you've lived a year of your life sleeping next to a fridge, you have no idea how much it changes you … or your diet!

Once we'd rented for four years in London, Rox and I finally decided to buy a place outside the capital and run off to Las Vegas to get married without telling anyone! About a year later, we fell pregnant with our first boy and, being blissfully unaware of what I'd let myself in for, I took the news much better than Rox, who spent a week thinking every pregnancy test she'd taken was somehow wrong!

After about a month of not really processing the fact that we were going to have a baby, I suddenly realized what was happening and started to freak out. Not only did I have no experience of, or any clue about, raising a child, but I also had no idea what it meant to be a dad. So I decided to set up a blog where I could document my journey into (hopefully) responsible parenting, and in the process perhaps find a few like-minded blokes going through the same life-changing experiences – and who might even become 'dad mates'.

Having never blogged before in my life (and being conscious of my dyslexia), I decided to keep things simple and name the blog LadBaby, as I was a lad and I was having a baby. The basic premise was to follow my transition 'from lad to dad' and prove that anyone can be an awesome dad if they put their mind to it.

For over a year, LadBaby was an online daily blog capturing the highs and lows of my life as a first-time parent – and then I decided to try my hand at vlogging. Almost overnight, my very first attempt exploded on to the social-media streams of people all around the world, and a simple video following my quest to replace my son's lost lunchbox launched LadBaby into the social spotlight. From that moment on, things have gone from strength to strength and our now-weekly videos featuring myself, Rox and our two lads reach millions upon millions of people and help bring a smile to the faces of parents far and wide.

LADBABY FACTS

- Mark is six-foot-eight and has to duck to get through doorways. Rox is five-foot-six and doesn't.
- Mark is a graphic designer and Rox is a full-time mum.
- Mark is 31 and Rox is 30 + 4.
- Mark is from Nottingham originally and Rox is from Kent.
- Mark designed the LadBaby logo from a side profile of Rox when she was pregnant.
- LadBaby first went viral on 11 June 2017 with the Toolbox Lunch.
- Mark never realized how much he said 'yes, mate' until LadBaby started.
- Mark and Rox's first son was born on April Fool's Day.
- Mark is a Nottingham Forest season-ticket holder. Rox only goes if she can blag a spot in an executive box.
- Mark's favourite food is sausage rolls. Rox's is vanilla ice-cream.
- Mark and Rox's boys are called Phoenix Forest and Kobe Notts.
- Mark won Celebrity Dad of the Year in 2018.

GAS, AIR AND EVERYTHING DOWN THERE

HOW TO HACK PREGNANCY AND LABOUR

BIRTHING HOPPER

ONE OF the first things you'll be told you 'need' to have in the later stages of pregnancy is a birthing ball to help you … bounce your baby out? Who knew, but instead of being conned into spending over the odds on a giant inflatable gym ball, just buy or dig out a trusty space hopper. Not only is it exactly the same thing as a birthing ball, but its inbuilt handles are the perfect thing to grab on to for stability whilst you sit watching telly … Oh, and it can even double up as a Christmas present for your kid in four or five years' time. WIN-WIN!

ROX: Definitely the most fun you can have in the early stages of labour! It made me smile every time I looked at it, and the handles were incredible for squeezing when the contractions got more intense.

BONUS TIP: Take it to the hospital with you on D-Day and it's guaranteed to lighten the mood as you bounce around the labour ward.

MIRROR, MIRROR

SO, YOU KNOW in films FBI agents use those little mirrors on the end of extendable sticks to look under cars for fugitives or bombs? Well, you can buy them from hardware shops for a couple of quid, and they're the perfect tool for expectant mums to have a look at what's happening 'below the bump'.

Whether it's checking out the state of affairs 'down below' during pregnancy, examining the aftermath once the final whistle has blown, or, indeed, searching for unwanted fugitives, the extendable mirror is guaranteed to come in handy from the first trimester to the third – and beyond. If it's good enough to sweep under cars for a bomb, it's good enough to sweep your undercarriage for a baby.

ROX: I have to admit, when I first saw this I was horrified. Surprisingly, though, it actually did come in handy for preparing my 'lady' for birth. It was also really useful after giving birth, too, when my midwife told me to keep an eye on how things were recovering downstairs!

PREGGO PICKER

FROM STRUGGLING to put on your shoes to reaching for the last bar of chocolate at the back of the fridge, spending months waddling round with an ever-expanding bump can be a right pain in the … er … belly? Almost everything you take for granted in everyday life becomes an uphill struggle when you're heavily pregnant: the bowling-ball-sized baby growing inside you makes its presence felt with every reach, bend or stretch. So what's the solution? Well, why not 'pick up' a litter picker for a quid from your local pound shop? Not only are they perfect for a spot of rubbish collecting when on community service, they're also ideal for helping preggos to reach everything they need with minimum effort. Trust me, within days you'll forget you're even pregnant … well, almost.

ROX: This became my third arm, especially over Christmas because it was perfect for nicking the best chocolates out of the Quality Street tin! You honestly don't realize how hard pregnancy is going to be in those final months until you find yourself struggling to pick up the post that's just come through the letterbox or battling to put your shoes on. Believe me, once you have this bad boy mastered it's a blessing!

WEE KEY

WE'VE ALL HEARD THE RUMOURS, but are they true? Would a police officer really hand over their helmet to a pregnant woman if she needed somewhere to have a wee? Apparently, according to UK law, if the situation demanded it, they absolutely would – though in reality, how forthcoming a police officer would be about anyone, let alone a pregnant woman, emptying their bladder into their helmet remains to be seen.

Did you know, though, that if you are a pregnant woman and you're worried about being desperate for a wee while you're out and about, there's a way you can access any locked disabled toilet in the UK. Just search online for something called a Radar key – it's a skeleton key of weeing wonder. So whether you're at a bar, in a restaurant, train station, coffee shop, shopping centre or supermarket, if you're bursting for a pee, you won't be caught short if you can't find a police officer nearby.

Just a reminder, these toilets are reserved for the disabled so we're only suggesting you get a key if you are pregnant, and that you use it when you are desperate to go and can't wait in the queue for the non-disabled toilets.

ROX: Just to clarify, I've only ever used one of these keys while pregnant, but my god, when you need to wee, like, a hundred times a day, having one of them to hand is the greatest thing ever. You take your bladder for granted before you have kids, but believe me, when you're heavily pregnant and waiting in a mile-long queue, you'll be thanking your lucky stars you have one of these in your back pocket.

CERVICAL PIE-LATION

THE INFAMOUS cervical dilatation guide is a glamorous piece of educational equipment passed around antenatal classes to help familiarize expectant parents with the stages of labour. It's an A4-sized piece of plastic showing how a woman's cervix gradually opens during labour until it eventually reaches a size when she can officially start pushing. Now, as useful (terrifying) as this chart is, I can't help but think it'd be a damn sight easier to get your head around if the sizes were translated into everyday objects we're already familiar with. So … please see my own guide below. Basically, nothing can happen until the cervix is the diameter of a microwave Chicago Town pepperoni pizza (other toppings are available).

ROX: Since Mark showed me this comparison chart I've not been able to look at a Chicago Town pizza in the same way.

BUMP-IER-MÂCHÉ

DON'T WASTE YOUR HARD-EARNED CASH on an overpriced keepsake cast of your bump when you can do one at home for free. Simply grease up your belly with Vaseline, mix some flour and water into a paste, then dip some strips of old newspaper in the paste and plaster them over your bump. Easy. Layer that bad boy up, wait for it to dry, then gently peel the whole thing off.

To be honest, the hardest part of this whole process was knowing what to do with a giant cast of Rox's stomach once it was done. Hmm, shall I mount it on the wall? Above the telly or the dinner table?

ROX: I have to say that at the time I wasn't a huge fan of taking a cast of my bump and boobs, but now I'm so glad Mark made me do it. It currently hangs in our spare bedroom and every time I see it, it reminds me of all the little kicks and wiggles our eldest used to make in my belly. It also reminds me how flipping hard pregnancy is and not to do it again. ☺

ELASTA-BELLY

IF THERE'S ONE THING about pregnancy you simply can't avoid it's your ever-expanding waistline (this hack was originally aimed at mums but if you're a dad who's eating in sympathy, this could be great for you too). As the weeks pass by you'll quickly notice that slipping into your favourite pair of jeans is becoming one of the biggest challenges of your day. At first you'll tirelessly persist at the expense of not breathing but eventually you'll surrender and either buy yourself a pair of preggo jeans that you'll probably only wear for three or four months, or consider the very real prospect of committing 100 per cent to wearing your pyjama bottoms everywhere you go from now on.

However, with just one elastic band you can (literally) extend the lifespan of your jeans and save yourself the potential embarrassment of showing the world your leopard-print Primarni PJs. Thread the elastic band through the buttonhole of your jeans and loop both ends around the button. SIMPLE.

ROX: A little tip is to make sure you're wearing a pair of high-waisted knickers if you're attempting this hack, as the last thing you want is your lady garden hanging out the top of your jeans. Just saying. 😄

LORD OF THE RINGS

ONE OF THE MOST important things post-birth is to make sure Mum has everything she needs for a speedy recovery. Having just spent a considerable amount of time in traumatizing pain, screaming at the top of her lungs and pushing a human life into the world, she's probably going to want (deserve) a few days' rest. Every man and his dog will have advice (ignore the dog's advice) concerning the best remedies for recovery but, whatever you do, make sure you get your hands on a kids' inflatable swimming ring. Don't worry, I'm not suggesting you take your nipper swimming on their first day in the world; instead, new mums can use it to sit on while they're recovering. Sitting can be extremely painful and uncomfortable post delivery, so this handy little life-saver is the perfect solution to help ease the discomfort and allow Mum to rest as much as possible. Oh, and of course it can still be used as a swimming aid for when you do eventually decide to take the little one for a dip. 😊

ROX: This was better than any gift or piece of advice anyone gave me after giving birth. It saved me from so much pain when sitting down and I'd advise every new mum to put this at the top of her post-birth wish list.

DON'T FORGET TO SHOWER

IT SOUNDS OBVIOUS, but one of the biggest money-saving hacks for expectant mothers can be to arrange a baby shower. Sure, it might not be the wildest party, when you're not allowed to get drunk, dance your ass off at a club and then scoff a kebab and chips in the cab home. However, on the plus side, your lovely mates will probably shower you with enough newborn baby essentials to open a small department store, from babygros and bubble bath to nappy creams and nipple creams … And yes, if you really want to, you can still scoff a kebab once everyone's gone home.

ROX: If you ask really nicely, your sister or best friend might help organize things so you don't stress yourself out too much.

SPLASH BACK

THIS HACK is probably one of the hardest in the entire book to achieve. It does, however, offer the greatest reward if successful. You may or may not be aware, but a number of fast-food restaurants, shopping centres, department stores, supermarkets and theme parks have reportedly rewarded families with incredible perks if the mother's waters break whilst on their premises: unlimited food passes, discount cards, huge shopping vouchers, and even free entry into venues for life. If you time it right, you could bag yourself a massive deal. The only problem … how to pull it off. Well, unfortunately I can't really help you with that, other than to say head to your favourite place on your due date and keep your fingers crossed – but not your legs!

ROX: Spending my days hanging out in Greggs wasn't exactly my idea of fun, but Mark insisted we should try, as he was convinced it would guarantee him a lifetime supply of sausage rolls if we got lucky.

GREGGS
Unlock
WE MAKE LUNCH
WE MAKE LUNCH
Vape Shop
E-Cigs & Liquids Sold Here

SIX THINGS TO PACK IN A HOSPITAL MAN BAG

THERE ARE A MILLION THINGS that can be packed in a hospital bag, but the majority come back home unused. It's not easy getting it right, but when you get it wrong it'll almost certainly be 4 a.m., your missus will be 7cm dilated, the midwife will be missing in action, and everything will be your fault – including the bottle of Lucozade she wants NOW but isn't there because she never actually asked you to pack it. Here are a few things not to leave home without.

01 ENERGY DRINK

If there's one thing to pack above anything else it's the supercharged maximum-strength energy drinks. Whether it's to boost the missus through the final pushes or to help you stay awake for a third consecutive day, you won't want to leave without them and risk missing something ... because she'll never let you live it down.

02 STARTER MILK

Whether you're planning to breastfeed or not, it's a good idea to take some ready-made first infant formula and bottles. Breastfeeding isn't always the easiest thing to master straight away, so a back-up bottle can be a real lifesaver. Not only that, if Mum has any problems and you're left holding the baby (literally) it's best to have a feeding plan worked out.

03 SNACKS

Pack snacks, snacks and MORE SNACKS. Hospital food is, of course, notoriously horrendous and vending machines are hit and miss (if they're even working at all). Stock up on all your favourites and remember to ration them: eating three tubes of Pringles in the first hour you're on the labour ward won't do anyone any good.

04 CAMERA

Sounds an obvious one but make sure you've got a decent camera to capture the first moments after your baby's arrival in the world. Whether you fancy yourself as an amateur photographer or are someone who just uses their phone to take photos of their dinner, this is one of life's greatest moments and you'll want to have it on record.

05 PHONE CHARGER

With every friend, relative, neighbour, work colleague and local corner-shop owner waiting to hear about the new arrival, you'll want to make sure your phone is fully charged and ready for action. Trust me, NO ONE wants their battery to die and then be turning their phone back on to twenty-nine voicemails from the mother-in-law.

06 LOOSE CHANGE

Sounds like a random one, but please pack at least twenty quid's worth of change for when you get to the hospital. From parking the car to buying cups of tea, hospitals run on change. With most labours starting in the evening, the last thing you want to be doing is running around looking for change for the parking meter when all the shops are closed.

NEW KID ON THE BLOCK

HACKS FOR HANDLING A NEWBORN

BABY MAN-SLIN

IF YOU'RE NOT ALREADY ACCUSTOMED to the world of baby products, you might find yourself getting lost in much of the marketing mumbo-jumbo. For some bizarre (money-making) reason, the baby industry has a habit of renaming everyday things to make them sound more important … and so they can charge you three times as much for them. Take a muslin, for example, which is apparently an essential item for cleaning up sick, catching dribbles of milk and generally wiping up mess. Otherwise known as: a cloth. Don't be conned into buying what are essentially flimsy, expensive tea towels – just use what you've already got. Better still, do what I did and find out if the local boozer has any spare (new) bar towels. They're designed specifically for catching spilt liquid and will stop you looking like a wet blanket.

ROX: Don't worry, I made sure the bar towels were new ones that weren't drenched in twenty years' worth of stale beer! As much as I hated them they've actually come in handy around the house a few times, mainly for soaking up the coffee I normally spill most mornings. 🙈

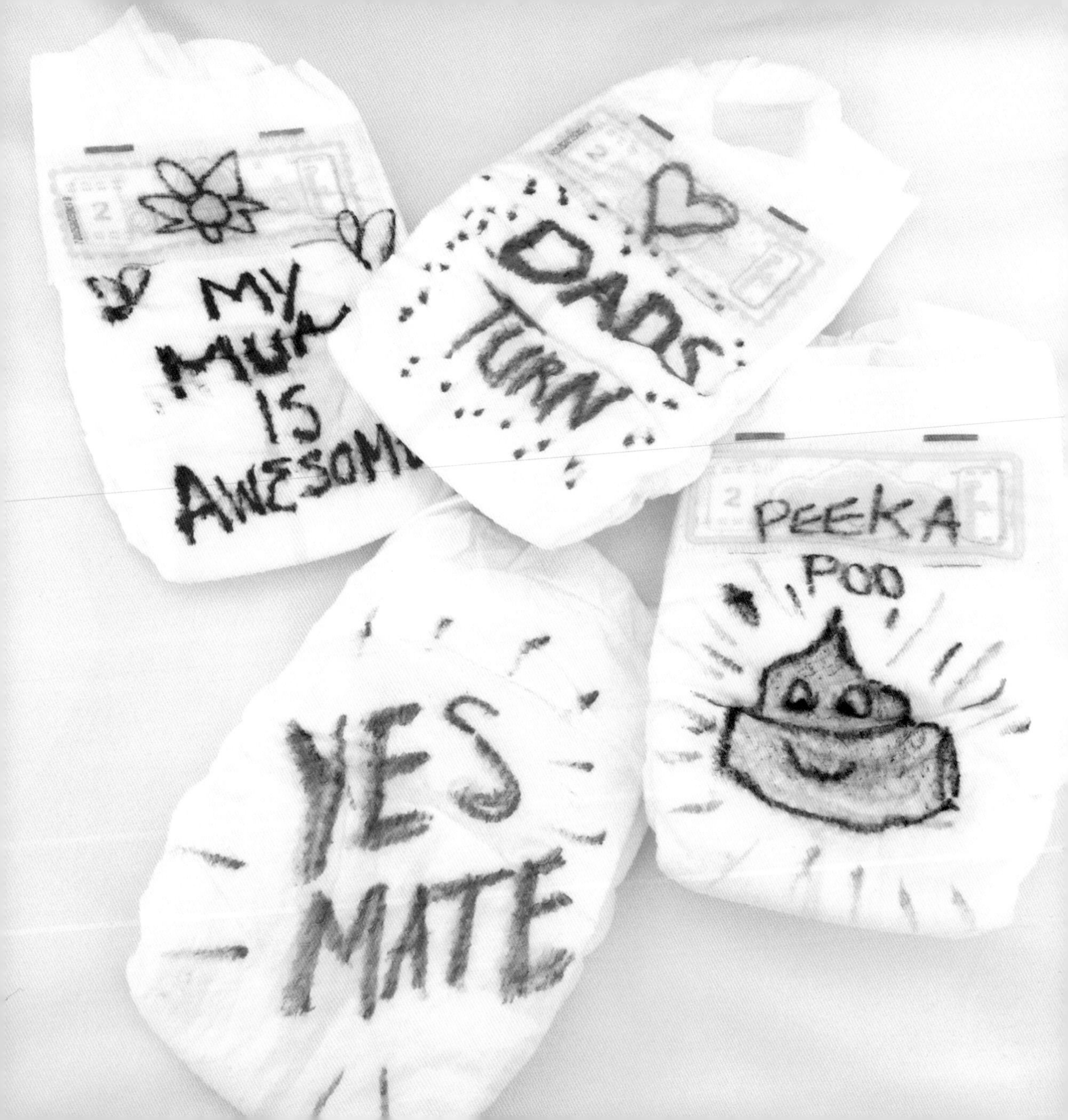
MY MUM IS AWESOME
DADS TURN
YES MATE
PEEK A POO

NAPPY POO-DLES

FROM NAPPIES with fancy covers to those with designer patterns, there are plenty of ways you could waste an absolute fortune on this basic piece of kit. However, here's one way to jazz up your kid's nappy without it costing the earth. Simply grab a couple of felt-tip pens and get down to business! Whether it's an inappropriate message for your partner to enjoy during a middle-of-the-night nappy change, a list of household chores for you to remember to do during the day, or simply an unexpected way of giving yourself a laugh, nappies are the perfect place to let your creative juices flow.

ROX: One dark and horrid sleepless night, not long after first becoming parents, it was my turn to change the baby's nappy at about three in the morning. I found one of Mark's rather explicit nappy doodles when I undressed the baby ... and I can honestly say I've never laughed so much in my life. Parenting can be tough but laughter can get you through some of the hardest days – and nights. I can't recommend it enough!

BABY SPRAIN

HAVE YOU EVER WATCHED one of those World's Strongest Man competitions on the telly, where some huge bloke carries a cement boulder the size of a gym ball round an assault course? Imagine how his arms must feel at the end of it! After twenty-four hours of holding, rocking, burping and tickling your child this is exactly how your arms will feel (only the cement boulder won't try to kick you in the shins every time you put it down). No matter how big or small your baby is, the daily routine will leave you feeling as if you've gone fifteen rounds with Mike Tyson. But is there anything you can do other than hit the protein shakes or inject shots of adrenaline into your eyeballs? Well, why not just buy yourself a couple of cheapo wrist protectors? They're probably not going to solve the problem completely … but they'll certainly give you a fighting chance.

ROX: Nothing or no one warned me of the strain having a six-foot-eight man's baby would put on my body, especially on my arms and wrists! Our eldest grew so quickly it was impossible for my body to keep up, so Mark bought me these wrist guards and they instantly eased the pressure. If your baby's a whopper, the sooner you get some the better!

Artwork by Alex Odisy.
Location: Blue Dragon
Tattoo Studio, Brighton.
Reproduced with thanks.

PICTURE PERFECT

DON'T BE CONNED into spending hundreds of pounds on a professional newborn baby shoot when you can create an ultra-trendy, Insta-mum-style photo shoot using nothing more than the camera on your phone and a wall. I'm not sure when it became the norm for parents to spend a few hundred quid on having their newborn photographed lying in a plant pot, sitting on a bookshelf or sprawled across a fluffy blanket, but the photography world is certainly glad that it has.

If you're not careful you could end up shelling out an entire month's wages on a USB stick of shots you'll never look at, an A4-sized canvas that'll need updating in three months and a digital photo frame you'll never remember to charge. Save yourself the expense by finding a wall covered in cool graffiti to use as your backdrop and organize your own shoot. The photos will be far more interesting than everyone else's, you can take as many as you want and, best of all, it's absolutely free.

ROX: I've always been more interested in these arty shots than the cheesy studio ones you can get done. Also, if you take your kid back to the same spot every year you can do amazing comparison photos! It's one of the best ways to gauge how much your baby's grown and changed.

DRIED SON

IF YOU EVER FIND YOURSELF in a baby-changing room looking for a hassle-free solution to drying off a wet child, look no further than the Airblade hand dryer! It's the perfect size and shape for little legs (assuming your baby is actually little!) and within ten seconds everything should be bone-dry. Before you panic, the air isn't hot and the noise it makes isn't that loud so the baby won't mind a bit. This hack might not be for every baby (or parent) but it works for us! It's so effective, I might start drying some of my own parts in it … depending on what fits. 😄

ROX: Mark just randomly did this one Saturday afternoon when he was out solo parenting! You can probably imagine my response, but apparently it was my fault anyway as I'd 'forgotten to pack the baby a spare pair of trousers'. Anyway, it turned out to be a great idea and now I do it all the time.

BABY LONG-LEGS

ONE OF THE MOST ANNOYING and expensive things about babies is the rate at which they grow. At first, you'll be impressed at how quickly your little champion can wolf down milk and double in weight within a few short months … but then you realize that all those epic little outfits you've forked out for are suddenly on the small side. Fear not. Next time you're dressing your kid and realize your favourite babygro doesn't quite fit any more, instead of packing up a bag for the charity shop just pick up a pair of scissors, cut the feet off (the outfit not the baby) and Bob's your uncle, it's just been given a new lease of life (for a couple of weeks).

ROX: If you're planning on having any more children perhaps don't cut the feet off all your babygros, as you won't be able to reuse them. Or you'll end up spending a fortune on socks …

SUPERMARKET WEIGH-IN

BEING A WORKING PARENT IS TOUGH, especially as you can sometimes feel as if you're missing out on seeing your kids growing up. Of course you're working hard to give them the very best start in life, but why should you miss out on seeing your baby develop? After all, it's just this sort of thing that makes the hard work feel worthwhile and creates the memories that you'll cherish for a lifetime.

Here's a solution: arrange your own baby weigh-in sessions at the local supermarket. Most supermarkets have the perfect weighing scales in their fruit and vegetable section, so make it a weekly ritual to pop along (no need to book) and place your bundle of joy (fully clothed) on the scales for a little update. Not only will you be able to monitor their weekly growth, but if you also select your favourite fruit or vegetable while your baby is on the scales, you'll get a little sticker to commemorate the date and their weight.

ROX: I loved doing this so much. Mark and I would do it every week when people weren't looking. We've got an entire keepsake book of fruit stickers at home and we get it out and laugh at it all the time.

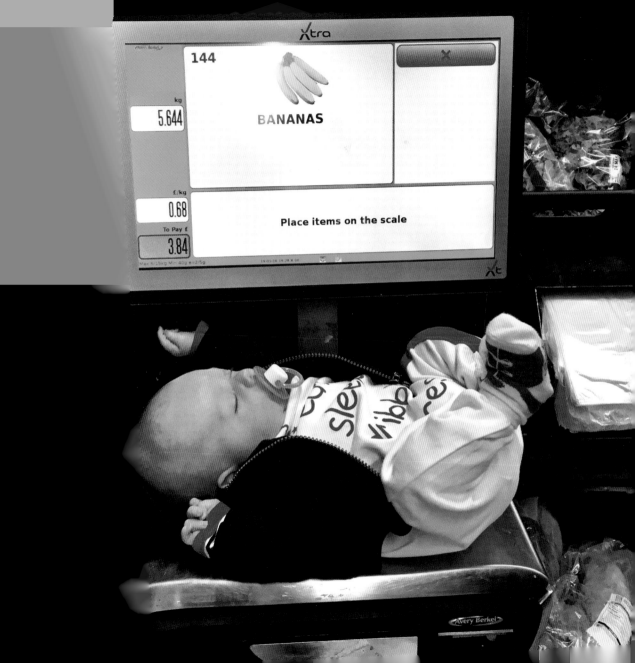

WHINE STATION

ONE OF THE MANY ACCESSORIES you acquire with the arrival of a new human is a changing bag, crammed with everything from spare nappies and wet wipes to clean pairs of socks and emergency pants (for you and the kid). Depending on your budget and taste in fashion, this lovely little baby 'essential' can set you back anywhere in the region of £30 to £150. Yep, that's right, £150 for a bag designed to basically help you change a baby's arse. If you want to keep things simple and save yourself a few quid, look no further than the booze section in your local supermarket. Cardboard bottle carriers are stored on the end of most drinks aisles and not only are they the perfect way to carry your beers home but they also make an ideal nappy-changing station with inbuilt compartments! No set-up time required, easily replaced when damaged and 100 per cent FREE!

FILLING YOUR NAPPY STATION

- Wet wipes
- Spare nappies
- Sudocrem
- Nappy bags
- Bottle of Calpol
- Sterilized baby bottle
- Spare clothing
- Beer/wine
- Beer towel
- Phone charger

ROX: This was genius! In the early weeks of parenting we had two or three of these set up round the house as emergency changing stations, so that no matter how tired or exhausted we were we had everything we needed in each main room of the house. Anything to save energy is worth it!

MOSES BUCKET

I DON'T KNOW ABOUT YOU but paying £200 for a Moses basket for a newborn to sleep in for a matter of weeks strikes me as ridiculous. How can a miniature bed be the same price as an actual full-size bed? What am I missing? Thankfully I've found a hack that'll save you a ton of money. Simply head down to your local hardware shop and for £4 (yep, just £4) you can get your hands on the perfect Moses basket in the form of an oval-shaped flexible plastic bucket. It comes in a variety of sizes, it's made from BPA-free plastic and even has built-in handles for easy transportation. All you need to finish the job is a well-fitting cot mattress and a couple of baby blankets. All in all, you'll easily be saving yourself at least £100.

ROX: The biggest problem with a Moses basket for me was that my baby hated sleeping in it so it was never used. This idea of Mark's is great because the bucket is light and easy for mums to move about in the first few weeks after giving birth. If the worst happens and your baby doesn't like it you can just use it for toy storage or as a secondary washing basket!

A GIFT
for your little one
GIFT CARD
For terms & conditions please see overleaf
Includes a gift envelope
IN STORE
FOR You x
USE IN-STORE OR ONLINE
GIFT VOUCHER
Spare parts

SH
REG 12-21
CLERK 2

1 MISC.
1 STUFF
SUBTOTAL
TAX
TOTAL
CASH
CHANGE

THE GIFT THAT KEEPS ON GIVING

NOW, I KNOW IT'S FROWNED UPON, is sometimes considered rude and even runs the risk of offending Auntie Linda, but returning stuff that's been bought for you and exchanging it for what you actually want can really be a money-saving game-changer. Don't get me wrong, you might want a third changing mat, a second baby monitor, a fluorescent lime-green pair of baby shoes or a six-foot stuffed toy giraffe … but if you don't, just return it! Most presents you'll be given will (hopefully) still have the tags on, and although you might be missing the ever-important gift receipt, the majority of places will still offer you a voucher or store credit in exchange for the unwanted item. EASY! All you then need is a convincing reason as to why you're returning it.

ROX: Mark's totally right on this one! You might feel guilty but if something doesn't fit or isn't to your taste, you shouldn't feel bad about exchanging it for something you really do want.

SIX THINGS YOU CAN DO, EVEN WITH A BABY

BECOMING A PARENT changes your life for ever but that doesn't mean you have to kiss goodbye to all your hobbies and interests. The minute you're given a child, you don't instantly turn into some old fart who likes reading the property section of the newspaper and listening to Classic FM, so here's a short list of awesome stuff you can still do, even with a baby. Remember, the kid's joined your life, not the other way round.

01 BABYSTATION

Believe it or not, playing video games actually isn't that difficult with a baby … as long as you don't mind multi-tasking. All you've got to do is master the art of getting your baby to fall asleep on your chest and then you'll have your arms completely free to save the planet, start a war or thrash a couple of mates on FIFA.

02 ARCADING

The lights and sounds of an arcade offer the perfect sensory session for your kid and the ideal place for you to let off some steam. Strap them to your chest, grab yourself twenty quid's worth of change and off you go. You can even attempt to impress your kid by winning them a soft toy from the claw machine. But I wouldn't make promises you can't keep …

03 PARK LIFE

It isn't up everyone's street, but if you're a fan of country strolls, hiking adventures and treks round the park then there's no reason to stop doing those things. Kids love the outdoors (provided it's not tipping it down) and the fresh air is guaranteed to tire them out. Personally, hiking isn't really my idea of fun … but walks through the park for ice-cream certainly are!

04 SHOPAHOLIC

Whether it's window shopping for clothes or pricing up a new lawnmower, if shopping is how you get your kicks that's no problem. While they're young, babies won't mind where they go as long as you can still feed and hold them. When they get bigger, just make everything a game. For instance, hide-and-seek is great when you're shed shopping. 😉

05 PINT SIZE

Probably my favourite piece of advice in the whole book: if you LOVE going to the pub and don't mind drinking responsibly, there's no reason why you can't still go with a baby. Most boozers are warm, friendly and full of comfy sofas, so get yourself a beer, find a quiet corner and make yourself at home. Just don't take off your trousers …

06 KICKABOUT

If you're keen on your sport and hoping to raise the next Andy Murray, Lewis Hamilton or David Beckham, why not start them young and get them involved with your kickabouts down the park. You'll probably have to wait a few years before they can be trusted behind the wheel of a car, but there's no reason you can't start teaching them the basics of football.

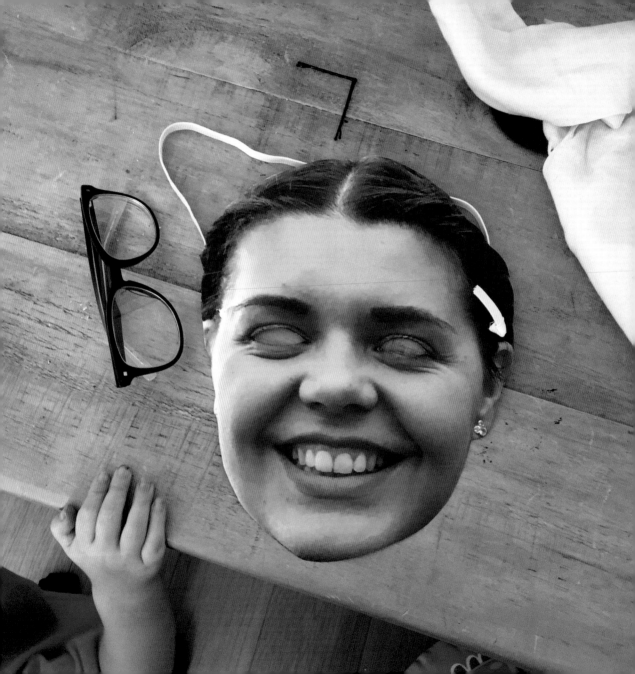

FROM DUSK TILL DAWN

COPING WITH SLEEP DEPRIVATION

DOG BED

PROBABLY THE BIGGEST CHALLENGE facing all new parents is sleep, or lack of it ... and the baby industry knows it! It preys on the weak and sleep-deprived, knowing that tired, caffeine-fuelled parents will buy absolutely anything in a desperate attempt to bag themselves five minutes' kip. One of the biggest rip-offs you'll encounter is a portable baby bed, aka a flimsy mattress and pillow shaped like a squashed doughnut that costs £150, or more. That's right, £150 ... FOR A PILLOW!

Thankfully, there's another item on the market that's exactly the same size and shape as the portable bed. It costs one-tenth of the price and has already been proven to be the perfect place for a daytime nap: a dog bed! Not only do they come in a variety of sizes to accommodate your growing baby, once you've fitted a sheet over it no one will ever know the difference!

ROX: I was absolutely horrified when Mark came home with a dog bed for our boy to sleep in, but I've got to say, he never slept so well. Don't get me wrong, I always made sure one of his sheets was down first, but credit where it's due, it worked out a treat and saved us a fortune. Mark also bought him a bigger one when he grew out of the first.

PET B

MODERN S

28"x 20

SLEEPYHEAD

IF YOU'RE LOOKING FOR A PLACE TO SNAG a crafty impromptu nap, look no further than your car. No matter how well stocked you are as parents, your partner will inevitably send you out on a supply run for milk, bread and a gallon of coffee. So when they do, make sure you're prepared by hiding a secret travel pillow in your car. Then race down to the shops, run round and collect everything in record-breaking time, dart back to your car and grab a quick thirty-minute snooze. This little power nap will then have you returning home feeling recharged and rejuvenated, ready to tackle an afternoon of parenting like a boss. Oh, just remember to set an alarm on your phone when you doze off … no amount of roadworks can explain a four-hour trip to your local supermarket.

ROX: Cheeky git, I always wondered why it took forty minutes to get a loaf of bread when we live two minutes from the supermarket!

MUM-MASK

AS A PARENT, one of the many problems you'll face at some point is your kid being ultra-clingy. Whether it's to Mum or to Dad, it can be incredibly difficult to maintain any sort of normal life when your child superglues themselves to your arms or has a full-blown meltdown every time your partner leaves the house … ESPECIALLY if they're the one normally on bed-time duty and you're covering that shift.

Save yourself the verbal, physical and emotional stress by making yourself a mum-mask (or dad-mask) that you can wear while your partner's out. The process couldn't be easier: simply print out a life-size picture of their face, cut the eyes out (I know this'll feel like you're acting out a scene from a horror film but stick with it) and wear it like a mask by securing it round your head with a piece of string. I know it sounds odd but, believe me, wearing it whilst rocking a baby to sleep can save your bacon.

ROX: I still can't believe this worked! It's probably the freakiest thing Mark has ever done … and that's saying something. The only disappointment was that s/he didn't do the washing, cleaning and cooking whilst I was out!

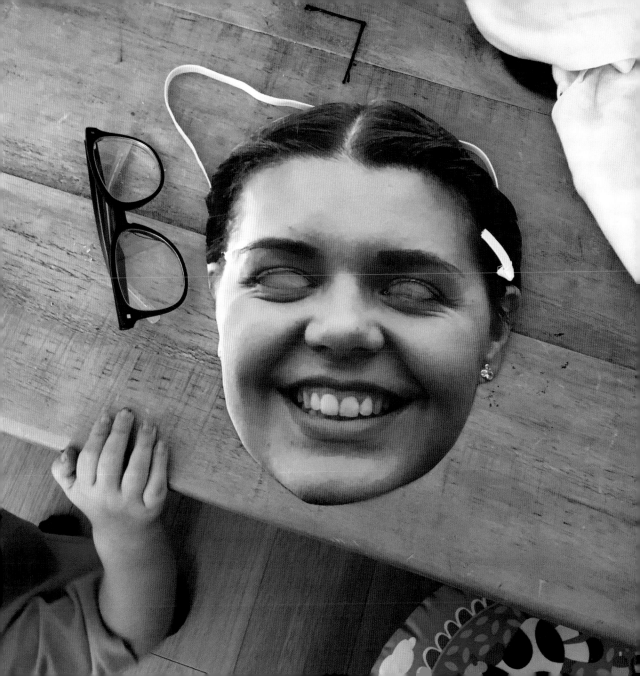

MARIGOLD MUM

GOT A KID WHO WANTS YOU TO STAY with them all night and goes mad every time you leave the room? May I introduce you to the Marigold Mum. First things first, go out and buy yourself a pair of rubber gloves (I suggest splashing out on new ones and not using the pair you keep under the sink for cleaning the toilet). Next, take one of the gloves and fill it with something to pad it out: toilet paper, kitchen roll or a pair of (clean) socks. Now wait until you're standing arched over your fidgeting kid's cot, desperately trying to lift your hand off their stomach without waking them up. Without warning, gently and swiftly replace your hand with the rubber glove. Think of it like the opening scene in *Raiders of the Lost Ark*: a smooth transition means a clean escape; a poor fumble means crying, screaming, a wide-awake baby, and the next thing you know you're being chased down the hallway by a deadly boulder … aka your partner.

ROX: Never in a million years did I think this would work, but it totally did! How he came up with the idea I'll never know because we've got a dishwasher at home and never even use rubber gloves.

HAZARD LIGHTS

AS WITH MOST YOUNG CHILDREN, you might find that leaving a night light on for yours can really help them sleep better. The soothing, comforting, gentle glow of warmth as they fall asleep helps to reassure them that everything will be fine during the night and, should they wake, they won't be frightened by the darkness and scream for your attention.

However, that reassuring gleam of love and affection is slowly racking up your electricity bill as it's left on for twelve hours a night, seven days a week, 365 days a year. The solution? Get hold of a discarded traffic cone with a light attached to it (obviously not one that's in use, the last thing you want to do is cause an accident). Or better still, pick one up from an online auction site for cheap.

ROX: I can't tell you how many times this has helped me when I've wanted a wee in the middle of the night. I also can't tell you how many times it's helped me find the toilet after I've had a few too many proseccos!

BEER-BOX BED

IF YOU'RE STRAPPED FOR CASH and looking for a place to put baby for a quick snooze, why not try an empty beer box? Sure, it's not a long-term arrangement and they'll have grown out of it within a couple of weeks, but while they're still small and sleeping loads it's easier than walking up and down the stairs twenty times a day to put them in their cot.

It might seem weird putting your new precious bundle of joy into a cardboard box but the Finns have been doing it for years. In fact, the Finnish government actually gifts boxes to all expectant mothers as part of an essential starter kit for new parents. Sure, their boxes don't have 'refreshingly perfect' written on the side, but apart from that they're pretty much identical. Oh, just remember to stick a blanket in the base of the box – it's meant to feel cosy, not like they're sleeping rough.

ROX: A lovely wine or champers box is equally good for this hack, just so you know.

OUT LIKE A LIGHT

UNLESS YOU'RE FAMILIAR WITH NIGHT SHIFTS, online gaming or all-night partying, chances are your body's not going to be ready for the onslaught of hourly night feeds in the early newborn days. That seven-hour sleep shift you used to put in every day now feels like a distant memory as you pray tonight will be the night you might just get two hours of uninterrupted kip. Sadly, I've not got a solution to stop your baby waking, but this hack will hopefully help you nod off as quickly as possible once the feed is finished!

All you need to do is buy yourself one of those plug sockets that comes with a remote control and connect a lamp with a low-wattage bulb to it in the corner of your bedroom. Then, when your baby wakes up, you can use the remote to switch on the lamp, which means a) you don't have to get out of bed if you're co-sleeping, and b) you don't have to startle yourself and the baby by switching on the big light. As soon as the baby's gone back to sleep, you can switch off the lamp with your remote and hopefully the low-level light has only made you more tired. Winning.

ROX: I'll happily tell every mum on the planet this is the best baby gadget idea ever! Nobody wants to get up every few hours during the night, and with this hack you don't have to. The dim light means the baby isn't woken up fully and you get back to sleep as quickly as possible once you're done. I would say this is an absolute must-have! It's also great if you had a caesarean and have trouble physically moving!

SUPERMARKET SLEEP

THIS HAS TO BE ONE OF THE BIGGEST NO-BRAINERS in history but for some reason it's gone unnoticed for a long time! If you're a parent who dares to leave the house more than once a year to maintain just a slight level of sanity, one of the many dilemmas you might face away from home is finding a place for your bundle of screaming joy to sleep. You might be one of the lucky few who has a kid that loves to doze in their buggy or who isn't really fond of a mid-afternoon kip … but if you're not, finding somewhere that's not only quiet but also comfortable can be a real challenge. Thankfully, though, there are hundreds of beds up and down the country just waiting for your little nipper … in shop displays!

When your kid starts niggling for a nap or screaming for a sleep, head to a department store which has cots on display, pop your little legend down for a snooze and then take a seat on the rocking chair that's usually conveniently located next to it. Not only will your kid get a nice comfortable place to rest while you take a breather, but the store should also be happy, as it demonstrates that kids love sleeping in their products. WIN-WIN!

ROX: I still cringe about this. I can't think of anyone who'd try to do this but somehow Mark managed to make it work … on more than one occasion.

THE SLEEP EXTRACTOR

EVERY MUM, DAD, NANNY AND BABYSITTER will have their own (apparently foolproof) way to put a kid to sleep. Whether it's singing lullabies, gently humming, taking them for a spin in the car or just dosing them up with enough Calpol to wipe out a small rugby team (joking, obviously!), there's method in everyone's madness. But what really works? Well, having personally tried pretty much every possible tip, trick and hack known to mankind (including the time I walked the buggy round the block at 4 a.m. in my Rocky Balboa dressing gown), I've got to say that the best sleep aid money can buy is something you probably already have in your kitchen … an extractor fan. Yep, that noisy little device fixed above your hob, which is only really ever switched on when you're burning bacon, is the best household baby sleep soother you can imagine. The calming and consistent pitch of its white noise is guaranteed to get you (and the baby) yawning in no time. It sounds crazy now, but just you wait!

ROX: I had every white noise app and YouTube video saved on my phone but, honestly, nothing worked as well as this. Putting your kid to sleep in their buggy in the kitchen seems weird at first but after a while I just got used to it and would make lunch in there while the little one was napping.

ICE, ICE, BABY

BELIEVE IT OR NOT, the temperature of your baby's room plays a massive part in how they sleep. Apparently, if you can maintain their bedroom at 18 to 20°C then you've hit the ideal temperature to keep them neutralized for as long as possible. I'll be honest, in the winter that's pretty easy to achieve because you can just put on the central heating … but what on earth are you meant to do in the summer when their room's hotter than a vindaloo in a microwave and your cheap desk fan just continuously wafts warm air around?

Why not make your own cheapo air-con system? All you need to do is chuck a few ice cubes and some cold water into a bowl and place it in front of the fan. The fan will then blow a nice breeze around the room, cooling the baby down and saving you from spending the night perched over their cot, fanning them with a giant leaf.

ROX: This _really_ helped our eldest when he was poorly and running a high temperature. It's also ideal if they're suffering while they're teething or after their vaccinations.

SIX TIPS FOR COPING WITH SLEEP DEPRIVATION

WHETHER YOU'RE IN CHARGE OF HEAVY MACHINERY, are long-distance lorry driving or trying to make it through the day with a screaming baby, the advice is always the same: do not operate when tired! The only problem is … you can't pull a sickie when you're a parent, so you've got to suck it up and solider on! It's twenty-four hours a day, 365 days a year and (in legal terms) for at least eighteen years of your life. So, with that in mind, here are our top tips for surviving the days *and* nights.

01 CAFFEINE SLAP

It sounds an obvious one but that's because everybody knows it works so well! Whether it's instant coffee, family-size chocolate bars or endless litres of caffeinated fizzy drinks, make sure you're stocked up on the good stuff so you've always got a slap in the face ready for when you need it most.

02 READY-TO-GO MEALS

It doesn't matter if you're a master chef or a microwave maestro, make sure you've got some pre-cooked meals burrowed away in your freezer for the days your arse is stuck to the sofa. They're a great thing to prepare before the baby arrives and an even better thing to hit your family up for when they ask if there's anything they can do to help.

03 SHIFT WORK

If you're both struggling to get enough sleep, my advice is to divide and conquer! Work out alternate time slots for sleep with your other half, so while one of you is catching up on the zs, the other one is 'on call'. It's not always easy if Mum is breastfeeding but if one of you can stay up late or get up early to allow the other a bit of shut-eye, it can make the world of difference.

04 PRE-DRINKS

Not only perfect for when you're getting ready to head out and hit the dance floor, high-impact isotonic energy drinks are also a life-saver when you're on parent duty. I wouldn't recommend you make them your sole source of liquid intake in a day but combine them with coffee and you won't need to worry about dozing off any time soon.

05 SNOOZERMARKET

There's only one thing that makes being tired worse than it already is … being hungry too! Being knackered *and* hungry is simply not a place anyone wants or needs to be. My advice? Set up an online shopping account with all your weekly basics saved, so that even if you're too tired to leave the house, you can still get a chocolate-fix delivered to your door.

06 SLEEP BUDDIES

It's probably the one piece of advice you'll hear more than any other but that's simply because it's so effective. The minute your baby drops off to sleep make sure you hit the pillow seconds later. You NEVER know when your kid might decide to pull an all-nighter, so catch up on sleep at every opportunity. I know it's not always easy, but believe me it'll be worth it!

FAMILY ENTERTAINMENT SYSTEM

KEEPING THE KIDS ENTERTAINED ON A BUDGET

THE DECOY GIFTS

OH, THE JOYS OF BUYING PRESENTS FOR KIDS. You spend weeks of your life trying to find them the perfect gift that they'll love and cherish for years, and then milliseconds after they've opened it they've tossed it aside and are playing with the TV remote instead. Don't get me wrong, TV remotes are a lot of fun, but as a parent it's sickening to see the five-speed, wall-climbing, light-up, music-playing remote-control race car you've spent four weeks researching now sitting abandoned in the corner of the living room while your child giggles and screams with excitement at the buttons on the TV handset.

Next year, save yourself the money (and the heartache) and just wrap up and give your kid what they *really* want. A TV remote, a phone charger, a novelty pair of glasses or a spare set of car keys … I promise you they'll be happier and won't mind you spending the money you've saved on alcohol (for yourself obviously).

ROX: Make sure you get your kid a duplicate TV remote because fighting your toddler for the one that actually controls your TV every time you want to change the channel isn't exactly fun.

BUILD-A-DAD

WE'VE ALL BEEN THERE: it's the weekend and you're in a shopping centre. You're trying to have a nice relaxing day while making sure your kid isn't throwing themselves down every escalator in sight, when you accidentally make the schoolboy error of walking past one of those bear-building places (legally I can't say the name of the shop … but you know where I mean). Your kid goes charging in like a … well, like a kid in a sweet shop. Before you know it you're forking out for a bear wearing a spaceman's helmet, a denim jacket, fluorescent PVC trousers and a pair of roller blades because 'That's what they really wanted.'

   Then, just when you think things couldn't get any worse, you have to watch as the bear gets open-heart surgery, a probe up its arse and is 'brought to life'. BRILLIANT! A more economical alternative? Why not just buy a cheap bear elsewhere and accessorize it yourself? You can dig out all your kid's old baby clothes to use as outfits and get any face you want printed on to a cushion cover (it'll cost you around £20 online), then stick it on the bear's head. ☺

> ROX: Yet again another one of Mark's ideas which is as freaky as hell but somehow miraculously works. Our boy adores it, calls it 'Daddy', and runs around the living room pressing the 'yes, mate' voice box Mark installed in its hand.

BASKET BALL-PIT

NO NUMBER OF ANTENATAL CLASSES or parenting books can ever fully prepare you for soft play … aka child warfare. If you don't fancy subjecting your family to a germ-infested play area where kids jacked up on Slush Puppies kick your child in the head while their mum inhales black coffee and reads *Glamour* magazine, simply create your own ball-pit at home by filling a washing basket with plastic balls. You're not only recreating the same joyous experience for your little one, but you're also instilling in them a sense of excitement associated with a washing basket, which is only ever going to be helpful during the difficult teenage years to come.

ROX: I've used this hack probably every week since the day Mark invented it. Our eldest loves it so much that we've had to buy a bigger basket as he's grown from a baby into a toddler! As a bonus, it actually makes doing the washing more fun too!

BONUS TIP: Take the plastic balls with you when you go to the supermarket and fill a trolley with them to make a ball-pit on wheels. This should keep them quiet long enough for your partner to race round and buy the eight gallons of milk you'll need for the day.

TAPE TRACK

NEARLY EVERY MOMENT OF PARENTING small kids is spent making sure they're not shoving their toes into plug sockets, diving headfirst down staircases or lobbing your iPad into the nearest open toilet. You would (literally) give your right arm to have just ten minutes to prepare your fourteenth coffee of the morning and attempt to drink it while it's still vaguely hot (warm) (lukewarm) (not cold).

Let me introduce you to the Tape Track. With nothing more than a roll of cheap masking tape (picked up from a supermarket for less than a quid), you can create a mega motor highway in under a minute, no matter where you are. Simply tear off strips of tape and stick them to floors, tables or walls in parallel lines to start creating your roads – it couldn't be easier! Now just drop a few cars on to the 'roads' and I guarantee you'll have your kid hooked for at least as long as it takes to check Facebook. Oh, and if cars aren't your kid's thing why not try making a masking-tape catwalk, runway or even a balancing beam.

ROX: Mark would get up early before work and set this up downstairs so when I took our boy down for his breakfast he'd have something new to play with for the day. It always worked a treat and normally meant I got to eat my breakfast in peace.

BONUS TIP: Use the masking-tape trick under a table in a restaurant to keep the kid entertained while you eat out! Who said romance was dead?

WET NET

THIS HACK ISN'T GOING TO CHANGE YOUR LIFE, instantly save you thousands of pounds or revolutionize the parenting game for ever. What it will do is stop you from sitting arse-first on a large plastic turtle. Basically, next time you fancy a bath, instead of jumping straight in the tub with all your kid's plastic aquatic livestock and risking an embarrassing trip to A&E to have something 'removed', simply use the netting you've saved from a bag of oranges to collect, store, dry and hang all your kid's toys out of harm's way. It's cheaper than buying a specific bath caddy-type thing to store all the toys and – some might argue – even encourages healthy eating. Bet you never saw that one coming. ☺

ROX: I felt like I spent a good part of my life fishing toys out of the bath until Mark came up with this idea. The best thing about it is you can have several nets of toys so you can easily alternate them for bath play on different nights of the week.

SAMPLE SHAKER

IF THERE'S ONE THING that's universally known about kids – whether you've got your own or are just sitting in front of one on a plane – it's that they love making as much noise as is humanly possible! You can calm them, entertain them and even distract them, but the first chance they get to lob a metal pan across a room, aggressively drum a spoon against a wooden chair or sprint round a shop murdering a musical instrument, they'll grab it with both hands.

So, instead of wishing someone would pour superglue into your ears, just embrace the racket and make them their very own shakers from (unused) urine sample bottles. It's a damn sight cheaper than buying rattles or instruments and you can design them to make a variety of noises. You're guaranteed to have a couple hanging around at the back of your medicine cabinet from when you were pregnant so get filling them with stones, uncooked pasta shells or grains of rice – or anything else you find lying round the house. Everyone's a winner … apart from your neighbours!

ROX: Why kids love making so much noise shaking and rattling stuff I have no idea, but our little boy loved these! As a side note I'd just like to clarify that I made doubly sure Mark was only ever making them from brand new, unused bottles!

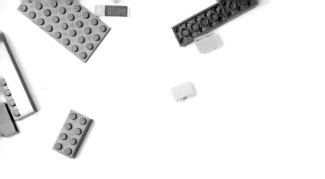
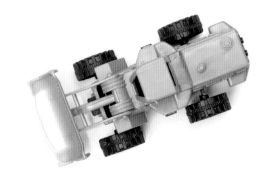

TOY RACK

WANT TO KNOW A CHEAP and effective way to store and display all your kid's favourite toys in one place so that they don't litter every bedroom floor, bathroom, hallway, staircase, and that place you once called a living room? Easy: buy a hanging shoe rack! You can pick them up fairly cheaply and, once it's hung up, it's basically a wall of easy-access pockets. It perfectly displays all the toys for mini hands to grab, it's more practical than a toy box because it can't be uprooted and swung around the room every five minutes and, best of all, if you hang it on the back of a door you can simply keep the door open to hide all the clutter.

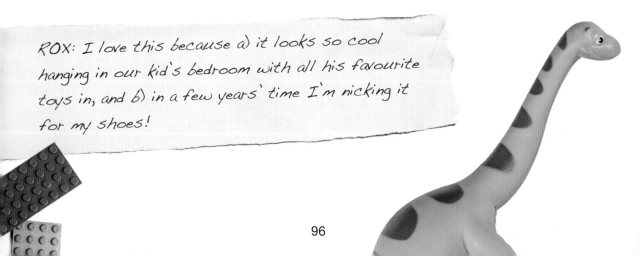

ROX: I love this because a) it looks so cool hanging in our kid's bedroom with all his favourite toys in, and b) in a few years' time I'm nicking it for my shoes!

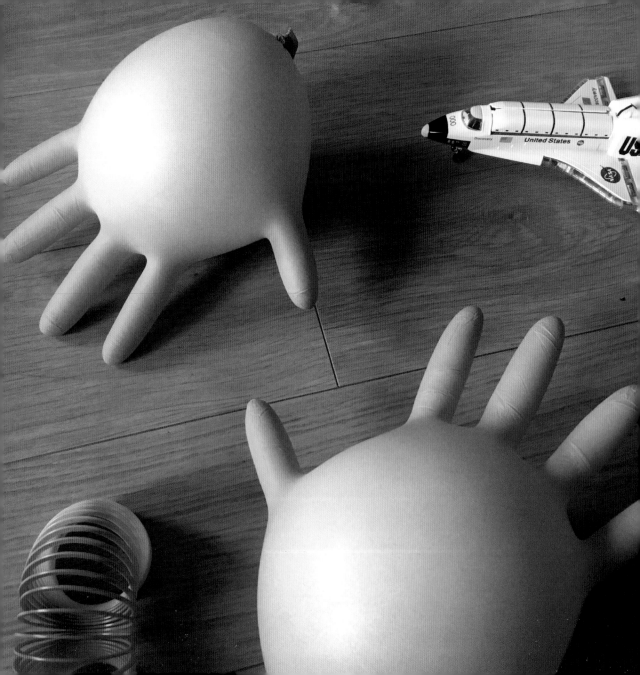

HIGH FIVES

DO YOU KNOW HOW TO ENTERTAIN your kid for free, give yourself a massive high five, a huge pat on the back and wave goodbye to an epic tantrum all at the same time? Simple, just get your hands on some pairs of surgical gloves and keep them holstered in your pocket until you're desperately trying to stop your kid from having a full-scale public meltdown in front of a crowd of onlookers. There's honestly nothing quite like diffusing a situation by inflating a rubber glove to amuse a whinging child. Whether it's in a waiting room, a busy supermarket or the lingerie section of a department store, I promise it's the perfect solution to make even the most judgemental people smile as your kid plays with an inflatable blue hand!

ROX: Every time Mark does this, I come close to wetting myself because I always think they look just like cows' udders.

BUBBLE FUN-NEL

IF YOU'RE LOOKING FOR A TWIST on an old-school classic that will wow the kids without you having to spend any extra cash, look no further than your kitchen cupboards. With just a plate, a funnel and some retro bubble-blowing solution you can create the biggest bubbles your kids have ever seen. Just pour some bubble mixture onto the plate, dip the wide end of the funnel into the liquid, then lift the funnel back upright and blow gently through the spout. It might take a couple of goes to master but once you've cracked it you'll never look at a funnel the same way again. *Boom*. Or should I say *pop*?

ROX: Mark and I get well competitive when doing this! We're both desperate to blow the biggest bubble and get the loudest 'wow' from our boy. Obviously I'm better and am the reigning Bubble Fun-nel champion. Just in case you were wondering!

ABC DIY

THESE DAYS IT FEELS as if some of the most expensive toys/games on the market are the educational ones. Whether it's counting, learning the alphabet, spelling, or mastering their colours, anything classed as an 'educational' toy comes with an inflated price tag … but why? Why should we have to pay over the odds to help the next generation learn the basics in life?

Well, now you don't have to, thanks to paint sample colour swatches. Most large DIY stores stock a wide range of paint cards and are only too happy to let you take home as many as you need to help you decide on the right colour for your imaginary spare bedroom. As soon as you get home, write the names of the colours on the swatches and you've just bagged yourself a set of colour flash cards.

ROX: I'm sorry, I'm not going to let Mark claim this as one of his own because this was in fact my genius idea! I'd seen the cards on one of our many weekend trips to DIY stores where Mark would drag me round, looking for parts to build the latest of his ' brilliant ideas'. Anyway, just wanted you to know because it's the best hack ever.

SIX THINGS TO STOP YOU GOING MAD ON A RAINY DAY

JUST A QUICK FYI, if you live in Florida or somewhere with nice weather this list will probably be useless to you. However, for those of you lucky enough to live in the UK where it rains 99.9 per cent of the time, I thought I'd put together a short list of wet-weather things to do with your kids to stop you from going insane and locking yourself in the bathroom to get some peace.

01 MAKING TRACKS

Crack out the poster paints and find some old toys to use as paint brushes and stampers. Whether it's old dolls used as long-haired paint brushes, cars pushed through paint to make coloured skid marks, or good old glow-in-the-dark stars used as stampers, get one last ride out of the toys to put a whole new spin on painting.

02 SHIPS AND DENS

It's an old-school classic but building dens, castles and spaceships with nothing more than a flat sheet and a duvet is still a winner. You can pitch your camp in bed, be a bit more adventurous and reign over a new kingdom with a sheet across the dining table, or blast off to an uninhabited planet by chucking a duvet over a clothes horse. The possibilities are endless …

03 BALLOON ROOM

This one involves a bit of preparation and a strong pair of lungs, but if you're willing to put in the effort the results are incredible. Basically, just blow up as many party balloons as you physically can (or until you pass out) to fill an entire room in your house. I know it'll be a nightmare to clear up but I guarantee it'll keep your kid entertained for hours.

04 BATH ART

If you've run out of paper for your kid to scribble on, or just want an alternative place to get creative with crayons, try the bath! No need to fill it up with water, just drop your kid in the empty tub and give them a pack of water crayons. They can scribble to their heart's content and when they're done you can simply wash it all off.

05 BOTTLE FLUTES

Want to make a kids' game that involves (you) drinking a few beers? Simply chug down a few bottles of your favourite ale, save the empties, give them a little rinse and then fill them up with different amounts of water. You've now not only enjoyed a few cheeky beers but also made a set of musical wind pipes!

06 BOARD

Whether it's Twister or Operation, everyone has a rogue board game or two kicking around the house. Dig them out and get the kids involved. Don't worry about rules … Twister is perfect for learning colours and Monopoly is ideal for making mini cities – and you can make epic houses from a pack of cards.

FEEDING TIME AT THE ZOO

HOW TO MAKE EATING A WHOLE LOT EASIER

CHEESE EDUCATION

IF ONLY THERE WAS A WAY to combine education with snack time. If only a snack could somehow help tiny minds develop with every mouthful. If only that educational snack tasted cheesy! Ladies and gentlemen, may I introduce you to cheese savouries. Normally found in budget shops or supermarkets in huge half-kilo bags, cheese savouries are pretty much made for educating (and eating while watching football). Not only is almost every savoury treat a different shape but some of them also match up perfectly with the four playing-card suits. First stop learning shapes, next stop counting cards! 😊

ROX: Only Mark could turn eating copious amounts of cheese savouries into a bloody game!

THE COLLECTOR

SO YOU KNOW WHEN YOU'RE DOING YOUR WEEKLY SHOP and you're annoyed that some snotty-nosed teenager hasn't pulled his finger out and cleared away all the empty fruit and veg boxes cluttering up the aisles? Well, now you'll be thanking that lazy swine as those empty boxes are the perfect feeding-time hack for the days when you just can't be arsed to do the cleaning up. Pop one of these empty boxes under your kid's high chair when they're troughing through their meal and it'll catch all the unwanted food that's spat out, thrown or launched off their plate. It's cheaper than buying specialist floor covers and easier than spending five minutes on your hands and knees scrubbing pie and mash off the floor. Just empty it into the bin when you're done!

ROX: This was such a good idea when we started weaning. Some days it felt like I spent most of my time picking food up off the floor, so being able to do it in just one clean sweep made all the difference.

ROLL WITH IT

WHETHER YOU'RE CLEANING UP SICK, a nappy explosion, muddy knees, snotty noses, chocolate-covered faces or scraping half-eaten shepherd's pie off the wall, the one thing you'll need more than anything as a parent is wet wipes, kitchen roll, tissues, takeaway napkins or handfuls of toilet paper, because EVERYTHING always ends up in a state. If only there were one tissue-related product that was capable of handling all of these situations …

May I present to you: BLUE ROLL, the undisputed champion when it comes to mess, madness and mayhem. Having spent years working in a supermarket, drinking in countless pubs, and living with a clumsy wife and overactive child, I can, without doubt, guarantee there is nothing blue roll can't sort. You can buy it from a hardware store for a couple of quid or grab a handful of the stuff next time you're in your favourite fast-food restaurant. Whether you've got a kid or are building an underground shelter to survive the apocalypse … make sure you've got blue roll!

ROX: I've ended up using blue roll for absolutely everything! Bleaching, dusting, cleaning, washing, wiping and even mopping. Mark's right, stock up for the apocalypse.

TOOLBOX LUNCH

YOU COULD SPEND YOUR HARD-EARNED CASH on an overpriced kids' lunchbox and cram it to the brim with Tupperware box inside Tupperware box, like some real-life game of Tetris … or you could head down to the local hardware shop and pick up a toolbox. Not only does a toolbox offer ample space to stash all your kid's favourite snacks, but it's also big enough to store enough food to feed a small army of tantrumming toddlers while you're down the park.

ROX: OK, I'll finally admit, I wasn't exactly convinced with Mark's toolbox lunchbox invention when he first brought it home, but I'm now happy to hold up my hands and say it's flipping genius! I still use it to this day and it's proved to be amazing more times than I can remember! Never in a million years did I think I'd married an 'inventor'.

BONUS TIP: Buy a double-sided toolbox and fill the other side with your kid's favourite toys. Now they can play and eat at the same time. WIN-WIN.

SUPER MUM

AS IF MUMS HAVEN'T GOT IT HARD ENOUGH already, carrying a baby for nine months and going through excruciating, mind-blowing pain pushing it out into the arms of a complete stranger, they then have to decide if they want to get their boob out every few hours to feed said baby. Of course, it's the most natural thing in the world to do, but I don't know how comfortable I'd be getting my crown jewels out in public every few hours, especially in winter. So I've come up with a little hack for any mums who might feel uncomfortable breastfeeding in public. It'll not only help them keep their style and grace but will also make them feel like a hero while they're doing it … A SUPERHERO CAPE! Keep your chosen cape under the buggy, then simply attach as normal and swing over whichever side you're feeding from to keep yourself completely covered. A small way to acknowledge the superhero status all mums deserve!

ROX: Everyone has their own opinions on breastfeeding but being a bit of a prude I found it really difficult to just whip out my boob in public to feed the baby ... Not to mention how I felt having to breastfeed at my father-in-law's house. So thank god Mark had this idea. It's made me feel so much more confident about breastfeeding in public and genuinely does make me feel like a hero every time I put it on.

FUNNY FOOD

DESPITE WHAT YOUR MUM MIGHT HAVE TOLD YOU, playing with your food could be a good thing! It could be just the ticket to help kickstart a change in habits for fussy eaters and save you loads on wasted food. There's nothing worse than seeing your kid turn their nose up at a meal you've just spent thirty minutes lovingly preparing and then watching as they flip their plate face down on the carpet. But with a few toys, creative noises and a loose storyline you can turn even the most unappetizing food into an experience to make them forget they're even eating their greens. (Honestly, the lengths some people will go to not to tell their other half they're a terrible cook is unbelievable.)

ROX: I love making themed food for our eldest! Dinosaur pancakes and dumpster-truck meatballs are his favourite. He engages with the food so much more than he does during normal mealtimes and eats twice as much in the process.

FAKE-AWAY

HAVE YOU EVER NOTICED that your kid never seems to complain about their dinner when they're eating a takeaway? Whether it's a burger and fries, pepperoni pizza or a bucket load of fried chicken, why is takeaway food so much more appealing? Well, in truth, it's normally because it's better. However, if you're looking for a cheeky hack to con your kids into eating home-cooked food, just remember to save all the boxes and containers from their favourite takeaway joint and then serve your home-cooked meal in them. I know you're thinking that it'll never work, but believe me, it actually does … and it's brilliant! Now all you've got to do is work out which one of your neighbours can deliver it to your door to make the lie completely seamless.

ROX: CONFESSION: I like putting my food in takeaway boxes when I'm on a diet because I want to try to convince myself I'm eating something naughty when I'm actually just eating a salad.

KEBAB STIRRER

YOU KNOW THOSE LITTLE WOODEN STICKS you get in restaurants, bars and cafés to stir your nineteen sugars into your fourth coffee of the morning? Well, next time you see them, make sure you pick up a handful because they're the perfect mealtime saviour when your kid is refusing to eat. Whether it's cereal hoops for breakfast, potatoes for lunch or fish fingers for tea, impaling food on the end of a stirrer will instantly make your kid twice as interested and can turn a repulsive-looking Brussels sprout into an exciting-looking new lollipop. Oh, and as an added advantage it even saves on the washing up. No cutlery required!

ROX: I'd also put pieces of fruit on the end of the sticks (slices of banana, melon, etc.) and freeze them to make little ice-cold fruit pops for when our boy was teething. Easy to make, great for chewing on and super effective at soothing sore gums.

PEEK-A-BOOB

AS A DAD, one of the many challenges you face with a newborn baby is that your body isn't, er, 'equipped' with the necessary source of free-flowing milk needed to satisfy your kid's hunger. Don't get me wrong, I'm not sure a set of boobs would necessarily suit new dads but the reality is, their absence can mean it's extremely difficult to help Mum with feeding time or give her a rest.

So here's a solution: find an old shirt you're not bothered about and using a pair of scissors make a small incision in the vicinity of one of your nipples (it's preferable to do this when you're not wearing your shirt). Pop the shirt on, grab a bottle of pre-prepared milk, then push the teat through the hole. BOOM! You've effectively just made yourself the perfect breastfeeding shirt. Probably wise to only use this at home, though, because it does make you look like a bit of a tit if you use it when you're out.

ROX: You've got to love Mark's effort in trying to hack not having breasts ... but I'm just not that convinced this one works!

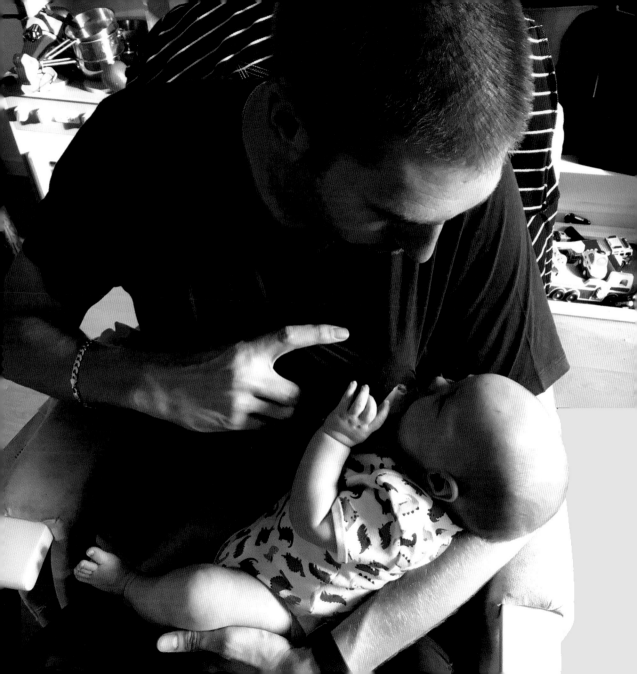

STACK AND FRIES

YOU KNOW THOSE REALLY ANNOYING, awkward-to-use little disposable paper cups for sauces that they have next to the straws and napkins in fast-food places? Although they're horrendous because they only hold a ridiculously small volume of sauce they are in fact BRILLIANT as a little pyramid-style stacking toy. Yep, just grab as many as you want, turn them upside down and then get going. How high can you make your tower? Well, that's up to you and how many cups you have access to. Strictly speaking I'm not sure how much the staff approve of this game but if it means you get to eat in peace who's bothered!

ROX: Any excuse for a McFlurry — I'm there!

Salt

Salt

SIX TIPS FOR EATING OUT WITH KIDS

THERE'S SIMPLY NO DENYING IT, eating out with kids can be one of the most embarrassing public appearances you regularly decide to pay for. Occasionally you might strike it lucky and get five minutes to scoff a club sandwich without chewing, but, nine times out of ten, your kid will probably sit there with their head spinning, screaming at the top of their lungs and wrestling to get out of their high chair as though they've been kidnapped by a stranger. So what's the solution? DISTRACTION, DISTRACTION, DISTRACTION! Keeping them entertained is your best chance of avoiding public humiliation so here are our top six tips to give you a fighting chance!

01 SPEED FEED

This idea isn't the easiest to set up but I promise it works! Instead of giving your kid the standard restaurant crayons and colouring sheet, why not take a car racing track with you that's small enough to fit on the table? You can set it up to wind around your plates of food and, though it's not the most peaceful set-up, you won't hear a peep out of your kid.

02 TABLE PLAY

If carting a race track around isn't something you fancy doing, don't rule out taking just a few of their favourite toys. I'm amazed how many people don't give their kids anything to play with at the dinner table. I know it's not ideal and you don't want them playing instead of eating but, I assure you, they'll eat more while they're playing than when they're screaming.

03 POPPING OFF

If there's one tantrum-killer and temper-defuser *every* parent, grandparent and babysitter should keep in their pockets in case of emergencies, it's an uninflated party balloon. Not only is it the easiest thing to carry around with you, but you'll also be 'blown away' at how it can stop even the worst outburst in its tracks when deployed.

04 iEAT

Others might judge you for it but letting your kid watch/play with a tablet at the table isn't always so bad. Maybe don't let them watch a compilation of *Die Hard* fight scenes, but what's wrong with allowing them to watch educational videos/games every now and again while they eat? Then maybe you and your partner can eat your food while it's hot for a change.

05 SACHET SELECT

It's simple but *sooo* effective. If you're having lunch somewhere that has a container of sauce sachets on the table, just empty them all out and get your kid to count them as they put them back in. Whether they're counting by units, colours or sauces, it's a great way to make an educational game fun while you're waiting for your food.

06 BOOTH BABY

If the restaurant you're going to has booths, always choose one. Whether you sit your nipper next to the wall or one of you sits either side of them, booths are a perfect alternative to a high chair, as you're still stopping them from running away from the table. It'll hopefully make them feel more grown up too because they're sitting with the 'adults'.

GO GO GADGETS

DIY HACKS FOR ALL THOSE BABY 'ESSENTIALS'

DIRTY MASK

WITH NOTHING MORE THAN A DUST MASK and a tumble drying sheet, you can save yourself the very real possibility of seeing your dinner again when you're left to single-handedly tackle an explosive, elbows-deep, upper-back, sack and crack nappy change. The smell and sight of such an episode is enough to turn even a pig's stomach and it's only once you're scraping shrapnel from under your fingernails that you realize you really are in deep … trouble.

To avoid such incidents pick up a cheap dust mask from a DIY shop for a quid and place a lovely-smelling tumble drying sheet inside the cup. Once fitted over your face, despite the horrors of what you're witnessing, you'll be breathing and smelling nothing but the sweet scent of freshly washed clothes … safe in the knowledge there won't be anything to hang out and iron.

ROX: I always laughed at Mark when he did this, and told him to suck it up (not literally). But when the teething nappies arrived I hated changing them so much I got him to make me one too.

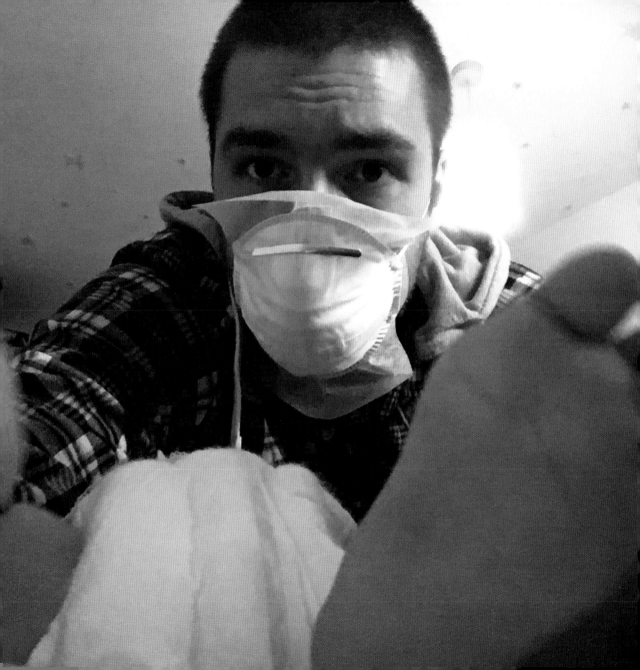

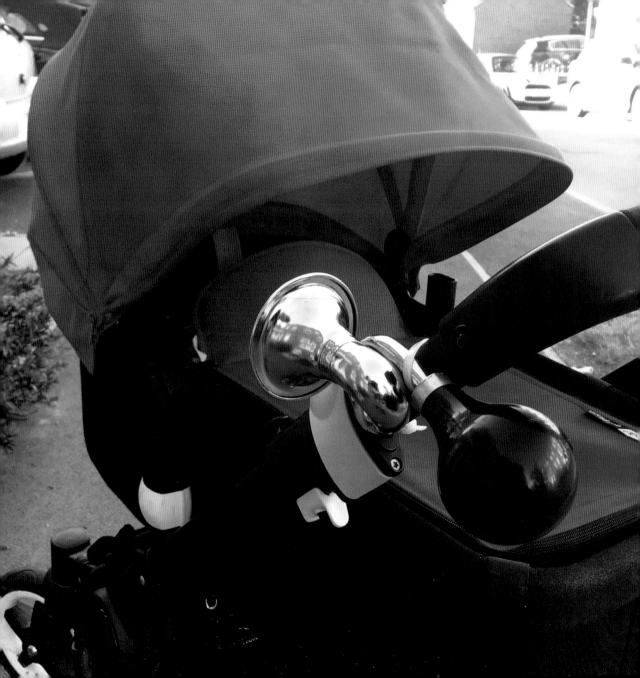

BUGGY HORN

IS THERE ANYTHING WORSE in modern-day life than getting stuck behind someone who's walking, driving or cycling at a snail's pace? I know patience is a virtue but at some point we've all just wanted to shout, 'Come on, mate, get a move on!' ANYWAY, don't think life will get any easier when you become a parent because you'll still be dealing with slow-moving people … only you'll be pushing a buggy too! You'll be trying to navigate the aisles of a supermarket, between tables in a restaurant, or along the pavement when some inconsiderate stranger will be going about their life in slo-mo.

To help with this problem, buy yourself the biggest and loudest bike horn you can find and attach it to the handlebars of your buggy. The next time you find yourself behind someone dragging their heels you can give them a short, sharp wake-up call to get out of your way!

ROX: I'm not sure what Mark's going on about here. I only remember him following me round the shops at the weekend, scaring me half to death by blasting the horn when I least expected it.

ZIM ZIMMER

YOU MIGHT BE MISTAKEN for thinking that once you've forked out for a cot, a buggy, a car seat, a year's worth of baby clothes and enough disposable nappies to guarantee a landfill site will be named in your honour, your bank account might get a bit of a break. But oh no, up rocks another problem – literally. When your kid decides it's time to make the evolutionary transformation from chimp to man (i.e. progressing from crawling to walking), it brings with it a new expense.

Instead of falling for the promises of the 'five-star-rated', annually awarded, 'number-one baby walker of the year', apparently proven to get your kid not only walking but also running faster than Usain Bolt, simply make your own from plumbers' piping. All told, it'll cost at least half the price of a shop-bought one and can be made to fit your kid's exact size and shape. Bespoke, I think they call it.

ROX: This baby walker got our son walking in one week. FACT.

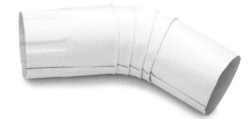

HALF DOOR

AS A PARENT, you'll spend months of your life trying to encourage your kid to walk and crawl. There's honestly probably no prouder moment in a parent's life than seeing your kid take their first steps. However, once the emotion and amazement have passed, the next thing you'll need to do is go out and buy stair gates to stop your toddler running into the kitchen and turning the oven on, or throwing themselves down the stairs.

There's one problem, though: stair gates cost an absolute fortune, especially if you end up getting them for the top *and* bottom of the stairs, as well as for the living-room, kitchen and bedroom doorways. Want to know what to do? Turn all your doors into stable doors by sawing them in half. As long as you make sure you cut above the handle, the bottom half of the door will still close and the top can remain open! PERFECT! You see, as one half door closes, another half door opens. ☺

ROX: No word of a lie, I was bloody fuming when Mark did this! He'd chopped my lovely kitchen door right in half and just seemed to think it was the most normal thing in the world. I always like to try to find positives from these 'challenging' situations, so all I can say is that it did make the kitchen look bigger ... And to be fair, it did actually work at keeping the kid out. I'm still not happy, though. Lol.

PIPE PROTECTOR

I DON'T KNOW WHAT IT IS about being naked that little kids enjoy so much, but sometimes trying to dress one is like wrestling an alligator that's constantly trying to perform a death roll on you. You've got to be able to move quickly and think on your feet, otherwise you could end up losing an arm. Or worse, you could get wee'd on. Unfortunately, unless you've got a Hannibal Lecter-style restraint suit (and mask) kicking around the house, you're not going to be able to stop the struggle. However, what you can do is stop them from hurting themselves in all the commotion. Just buy some cheap pipe-insulation tubes and pop them on to the edges of your changing table. The foam-cushioning will mean that even if they successfully execute the death roll, no one's going to be making a trip to A&E … Well, the kid won't be, anyway.

ROX: Sometimes I really do worry about what goes on in Mark's head!

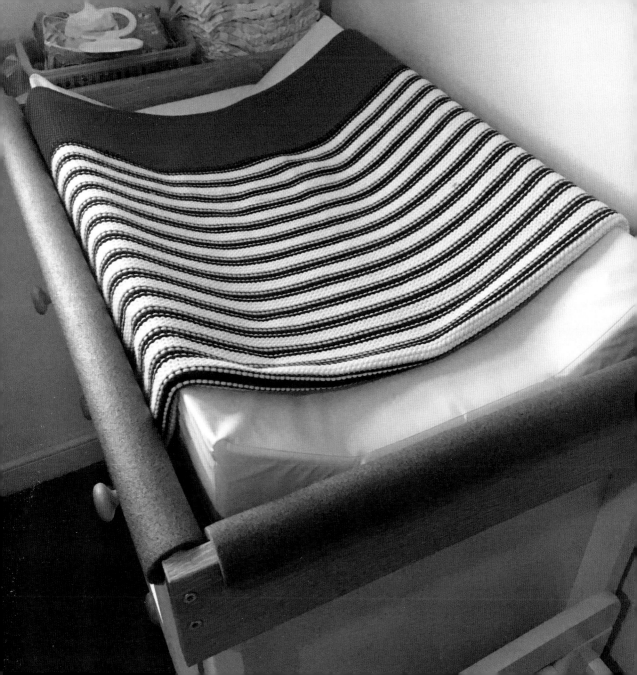

INSULATION DOOR

WHILE WE'RE ON THE SUBJECT of awesome stuff you can do with pipe insulation, let me tell you about this other epic little hack you can do with all the offcuts from the Pipe Protector on the previous page. It couldn't be easier, really: simply pop the insulation tubing around the bottom of a door (any sized piece should work) and you've instantly transformed said door from a miniature finger guillotine into a child-friendly, slam-proof safety one. The positive news is it's a damn sight cheaper than buying specialized door wedges. The bad news is that the next time you're having an argument with your other half and try to slam a door in rage, it just won't work and you'll end up looking like a massive prat. Just an FYI!

ROX: For some bizarre reason our eldest likes sticking his hands, feet and nose into every possible gap or crevice going, so this hack probably saved him from losing at least a couple of fingers.

THE BABY BELT

HERE'S A QUESTION I bet you've never been asked before: have you ever noticed what a perfect invention a toolbelt is? I mean, like, *really* noticed? Not only can you easily attach it to your waist but you can also use it to store everything you'll ever need for a particular job so that it's right there at your fingertips. Other than if you're rewiring a house or going to a weirdly themed fancy-dress party, can you tell me when else it would be handy to have everything you need, hanging round your waist? WHEN YOU'RE HOLDING A BABY!

Get your hands on a decent toolbelt from a DIY store (it'll cost you about £12) and fill it with every parenting essential you'll need to survive the day: nappies, wet wipes, Calpol, phone charger, (bottle of wine), nail clippers, and anything else you can think of. Now relax, you've saved yourself from spending at least £100 on a 'mums' awards' changing bag and have the solution to every baby-related problem hanging round your crotch.

ROX: When Mark had to go back to work after paternity leave, this was a life-saver! Some days the baby would fall asleep on me and, thanks to this belt, I wouldn't have to move! In a weird sort of way, it was like having Mark off work with me still, which was amazing!

MOTOR MUSLIN

DON'T WASTE YOUR TIME, energy or money on one of those flimsy blinds you stick on the inside of your car window to try to keep the sun off your kid's face. The reality is, they never stick to the glass properly, always seem to be in the wrong place to actually block out the sun, and eventually they end up flying out of the window on the M1 at 70 mph because you've forgotten it's there and wound down the window. Why not save yourself the money and hassle by just closing an old blanket/large piece of cloth in the car door. It might look a bit weird but I guarantee it'll block out twice as much light as one of those little blinds, with half as much effort. Sure, a blanket probably isn't the gold standard when it comes to UV protection but the British weather doesn't give us much opportunity to be too worried about that, to be honest.

ROX: This was super quick and easy to do and could be added to any of the windows/doors of the car, depending on where the sun was. We still had a clear view!

A HELPING HAND

NONE OF US LIKES DOING IT, and we'd all try to shirk it at the first possible opportunity. And if we could pay someone else to do it for us, we probably would … but unfortunately changing nappies is just one of the many glamorous jobs a parent has to do. Quite often it feels as if you're sticking your hands directly into a temperamental bear trap. Ninety per cent of the time you'll escape unscathed with your dignity still intact, however there's always a 10 per cent chance you'll get caught, be covered head-to-toe in human excrement and walk away wondering if you'll ever feel clean again. Disappointingly, I don't have a hack to avoid the nappy-changing ritual entirely, but I do have one to keep your hands clean: free plastic gloves from the petrol station. They're available at the pump when you're filling up the family wagon, so grab a couple of pairs and keep them close by for when you're in real … trouble.

ROX: Is this classed as theft? I guess they're free if you're filling up your car! Please, if you get arrested for nicking free gloves don't tell the police my husband told you to do it.

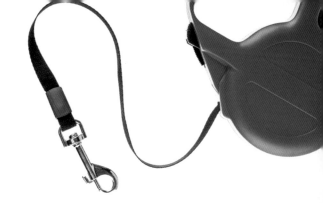

WALKIES

DEPENDING ON HOW LUCKY YOU ARE, using reins on your toddler usually goes one of two ways. Either they won't notice you've put the harness on them and/or won't care, or it'll be like you're walking the streets with a starving zombie you've kept captive in your shed for the last three decades as they fight and scream to break free. Unfortunately, you're probably not going to know how your kid will react until you've already spent the money and bought some … right? WRONG. Instead of splashing the cash on an item your kid might absolutely detest, why not just use/borrow a mate's retractable dog lead? You can simply clip the lead onto your kid's backpack – not only does it work in exactly the same way as kids' reins do, but it also extends a lot further so will allow your kid to feel less restrained and explore the world around them more freely.

ROX: The biggest problem we had with baby reins on our boy was that he hated feeling restricted, but he didn't mind the doggy lead one bit! I assume it was because he could roam around a lot more and probably forgot he even had it on … Either that or he just likes acting like a dog.

SIX PLACES TO FIND AWESOME SECOND-HAND BABY KIT

WHEN YOU HAVE A BABY YOU OF COURSE want them to have everything they could possibly need for a happy and healthy start in life. But that doesn't always mean you need to buy everything brand new. There are plenty of items you can get your hands on for cheap, which could end up saving you an absolute fortune in the long run. Some things might need a little wipe down or a dip in the sterilizer, but there are bargains to be had if you know the right places to look. Here are our top destinations for bargain hunts.

01 BABY BOOT

Above anywhere else, the one place you are guaranteed to find baby stuff on the cheap is a car-boot sale – it's *always* a winner. From travel cots to travel buggies, baby walkers to high chairs, I promise you that you'll head home with something costing you one-tenth of the high street price.

02 NANNY'S LOFT

You might not remember it, but your mum and dad were new parents once upon a time, and if you're lucky they *might* still have a few useful items kicking around in the loft. You're unlikely to find a car seat up to current safety standards (kids aren't allowed to just sit on bread baskets any more) but you're sure to find clothes, rattles and a host of other vintage toys.

03 THE MARKET PLACE

Facebook Marketplace is probably the best online tool for finding cheap baby stuff that's for sale right on your doorstep. Set your location, define what you're looking for, add the distance you're willing to travel and then hit 'search'. You won't get results every time but if Hannah around the corner is flogging her kid's travel cot you've not got to go far to collect it.

04 MATES RATES

Chances are that by the time you've decided to have a baby at least one of your mates will have already had one and will be further down the parenting road than you. If you know they're not planning on having any more, you might be able to prise some unwanted stuff out of them. After all, nobody wants their loft to be clogged up with too much old baby stuff.

05 eBABY

It's an oldie but it's still a goldie! Head online and try your hand at some online auction sites. Yes, someone might outbid you at the last minute and you'll lose something you really want *or* you could go unchallenged and pick up a buggy for next to nothing.

06 CHARIT-YAY SHOP

Perhaps the most obvious place of all, but if you're looking to grab yourself a bargain at rock bottom prices simply head to your local charity shop. There's at least one on every high street and on top of saving yourself a few quid, your money will be going to a worthy cause or someone less fortunate than yourself.

DAYS OUT OUT

A HACKER'S GUIDE TO FAMILY EXCURSIONS

PETTING ZOO

A DAY TRIP TO THE ZOO has to be one of the most expensive days out in modern-day parenting (followed closely by the cinema). I totally understand that looking after hundreds of species of animals can't come cheap but at least they don't have to be clothed for eighteen years, supplied with mobile phones and provided with a pricey university education.

Save yourself the expense of a zoo trip by simply visiting a local pet shop. Not only will the trip cost you nothing but most decent places will also let you stroke the animals, so the kids will get a more 'up close and personal' experience. I know seeing a rabbit isn't the same as seeing a lion but hold on to the fact that you're avoiding paying over the odds for nuggets and chips from the zoo café.

ROX: You can't compare goldfish and hamsters to tigers and elephants but the kid always seemed to enjoy our trips to the pet shop so I'm not complaining.

HERO CHRISTENING

IF YOU FANCY SAVING YOURSELF A FEW BOB on a christening and don't mind offending your uber-religious aunty, why not arrange your ceremony at the (steel) feet of a statue of your hero? You won't have to spend a fortune on hiring a venue, you won't have to pay an appearance fee for your hero to show up *and* you'll be avoiding the stress of organizing a seating plan by just telling people to join you at the statue ten minutes before kick-off. All you've got to do is set a date, tell all your loved ones to dress appropriately for the occasion (football shirt in my case) and then present your bundle of joy to your hero on the big day. EASY! Then you just need to decide where to go for drinks after!

ROX: Just to confirm we didn't officially get our son christened at the Brian Clough statue! At least I don't think we did ...

FESTIVE FORK-LIFT BUGGY

SO IT'S THE FIRST WEEK OF DECEMBER, which can mean only one thing … the annual Christmas ~~argument~~ debate: 'What size Christmas tree are we buying?' Well, before you start worrying about whether the 'perfect' six-foot Norwegian spruce your partner has lovingly spent twenty minutes choosing is going to fit in your living room or whether you'll end up cutting it in half (if you know, you know), you first need to work out how you're going to get it home, especially if you don't have a car.

Whether you hire a van or opt to pay the extortionate delivery fee the seller will inevitably charge you, it's going to end up costing you just to get the sodding thing home. (Unless you bite the bullet and tell your other half to buy a smaller tree, that is!) Instead, why not just strap it to the top of your kid's buggy (not while they're in it, of course) and just push it home! I can't promise it'll be easy but if you want free delivery, that's the price you'll have to pay.

ROX: I'm one of those people who starts to talk about Christmas in August, so seeing Mark coming down the road with a Christmas tree strapped to the top of the buggy and our boy laughing in the basket underneath was probably better than seeing Santa Claus himself! Absolute magic.

TROLLEY TROOPERS

WANT TO KNOW HOW YOU CAN SURVIVE a shopping trip with a toddler without wanting to jam your own head into an oncoming convoy of trollies? Simple: take them to the fancy dress section in the clothing department and let them choose a costume to try on from the range. Batman? Why not. The Hulk? Sure thing. Stormtrooper? Now we're talking! While you're pricing up the cheapest high-percentage bottles of wine, your kid will be saving (destroying) the universe. Oh, and don't forget to return the costume to where it came from if you decide you don't actually want to buy it after all.

ROX: Doing the weekly food shop is so boring but there's nothing I love more than acting like a big kid, so this is perfect. I just wish I could get dressed up as well ... but it'd probably get me too much unwanted attention.

DIGGER DAYS OUT

WHY IS IT THAT EVERY ATTRACTION, experience, event, day out and family-related gathering costs an absolute fortune to attend? If it's not the entry tickets ripping you off, it's the parking, souvenirs, restaurants, novelty snacks, in-ride photos and waterproof ponchos. If you're a family on a budget, the expense of going on a 'family fun day out' could mean you end up eating beans on toast for the rest of the month or selling a body part to science (if they'll have it).

However, you can avoid having to cook all your meals on a bonfire and save yourself a fortune by taking your family to an 'urban attraction' such as a building site. While obviously remaining on the safe side of the fence, you and your family can enjoy the thrills and spills of a live-action digger (or other large machine) but without a hefty price tag to match.

ROX: When you can't face another day in soft play this is such a fab thing to do. Our eldest is obsessed with cars and diggers so we regularly go and find cranes, trucks and other big machines for him to watch! Hours of fun ... for him!

SENSORY JACKPOT

FROM THE MINUTE YOUR BABY ARRIVES in the world, you'll be bombarded with a never-ending stream of invitations and recommendations for local parent–baby classes which you apparently need to attend to help your child's development. Whether it's baby massage (yep, baby massage) to help … de-stress your baby, or a sensory class to help … your kid develop its sensors? There's basically a whole host of people queuing up to take your money in exchange for thirty minutes of garbage in a local village hall.

Avoid falling into the new-parent guilt trap and, instead of signing up to a ten-week course of sensory classes, just take your baby to an arcade. The lights and sounds are enough to stimulate anyone's senses and, best of all, you don't even have to spend any money (if you don't want to) because the baby will be more mesmerized by all the flashing buttons.

ROX: Is there anything more fun than a seaside arcade? My folks used to love taking me on the penny slot machines when I was a kid and now I know why, because the minute you leave the arcade the kids fall fast asleep, worn out from all the excitement.

SHED GROTTO

IF CHRISTMAS IS AROUND THE CORNER and you've forgotten to put your kid's name down for a visit to 'the best Santa's grotto in the whole country', don't panic. I've got a hack that won't just save you a verbal battering from your other half but could kick off a whole new festive family tradition: the Shed Grotto! With nothing more than a few rolls of wrapping paper, some cheap decorations and a half-decent Santa suit, you can transform your shed (and everything in it) into the perfect festive log cabin. Don't worry about tidying and cleaning it out beforehand, just wrap everything in sight! From the lawn mower to the BBQ, once it's wrapped with snowman-patterned paper, the kids won't have a clue. Warning! Just make sure Santa knows where the real gifts are so no one goes home with a strimmer.

ROX: I think Mark's Shed Grotto is one of my fondest Christmas moments ever, and a memory I'll cherish for the rest of my life. Our kid loved it and we still laugh about it now every time we go in the shed!

WHEELIE SLEDGE

SO, YOU KNOW HOW WHEN IT SNOWS you want to take your kid sledging but you really don't want to fork out for a sledge that you'll probably use once and then leave to gather dust in your garage for the other 364 days of the year? Well, what if I told you EVERYBODY in the country has a sledge (or maybe three) outside their house already? Nope, I'm not suggesting you smash up your garden fence and slide down a snowy hill on a death trap, I'm talking about your wheelie bin! All you have to do is place a pair of pliers between the joins on the hinges and gently tap with a hammer. Do this on both sides to safely remove the lid without causing any damage and you'll find yourself with the perfect home-made sledge, complete with handles! Best to give it a rinse before sitting on it. 😉

ROX: How on earth Mark thought of turning a wheelie-bin lid into a sledge is completely beyond me, but worryingly it works surprisingly well.

CEMENT-IMENTAL

I DON'T KNOW WHEN IT BECAME 'the thing to do' but many new parents seem to like to get casts of their kids' hands and feet done. To be honest, it seems a bit weird to me, especially when you go into someone's house and catch sight of a pair of silver hands and feet hanging on the wall – but each to their own, I guess.

Anyway, if this sort of thing is up your alley don't get conned into splashing the cash for a 'professional' cast when you can do one yourself for a tenth of the price. Simply buy a bag of cement from your local hardware store, mix as instructed (making sure no one breathes in any cement dust), pour into your chosen receptacle (for example a large sturdy plastic container) and then plop your little one's hands and feet in. Obviously never leave them in there for too long and completely wash them down as soon as you've finished. Better still, if you're worried about your kid's skin coming into contact with the cement, simply put clingfilm over their hands. With the money you've saved, you can now afford to do a new one every year.

ROX: Doing this made me feel as if our boy was joining the Hollywood Walk of Fame ... only it was in our back garden, with cement Mark had mixed in a bin and without thousands of people clapping and cheering. It does make me smile every time I look at it, though.

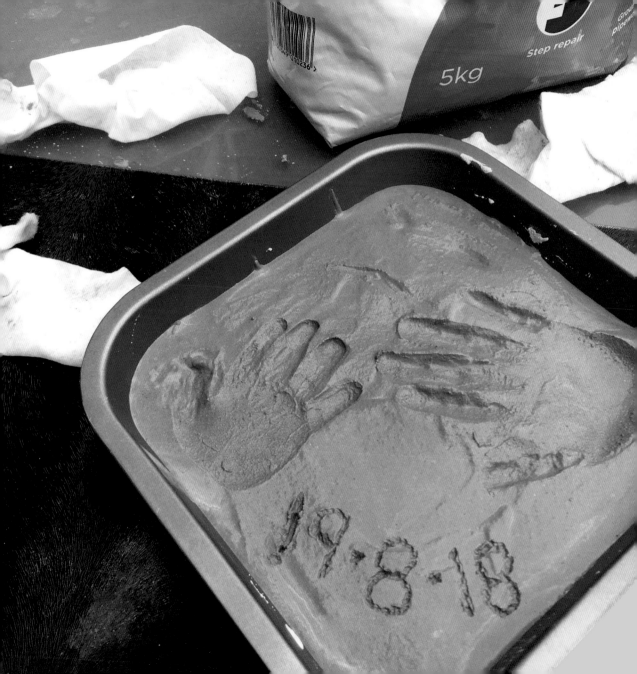

PIE SMASH

IT'S A CRAZY IDEA that I can only imagine was invented in the US, but now it seems that every man and his dog is organizing a cake smash for his kid's first birthday. I'm not entirely sure what the fascination is with watching a child badly attempt to punch a Victoria sponge but I suppose it beats a soft-play party.

Anyway, if your kid's more of a fan of savoury food, you don't particularly want to eat mushed-up birthday cake, or you just need an excuse to buy meat pies (not that anyone should need an excuse), why not organize a pie smash instead? It's a damn sight funnier than a cake smash and pies are certainly cheaper to buy than elaborate birthday cakes – plus, you can keep the birthday celebrations going by having pie and mash for dinner!

ROX: Doing this made me laugh more than it should have! Watching Mark stacking pies like the tiers of a wedding cake was a sight to behold!

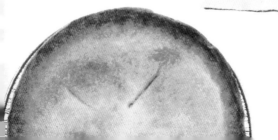

SIX CHEAP FAMILY DAYS OUT

WE'VE ALL BEEN THERE: it's the weekend before payday and although you're sick to death of being at home and the kids are climbing the walls, you can't go anywhere because you're totally broke. So here are six fun, low-cost places you can go to keep you from going insane.

01 SHOW-OFF

Instead of paying rip-off prices for entry into soft play, why not take your kid to a car showroom? I know it doesn't sound that exciting but, believe me, unless you've sat in a car you can't afford while your kid head-butts the steering wheel, stamps on the gear stick and punches the air-con system, you've clearly not lived.

02 BOUNCY BED

So apparently trampoline parks have taken over as the go-to destination for fun and excitement. I'd rather kick a ball around a field than jump on the spot in a sweat warehouse, but what do I know? If your kid loves bouncing around, why not just take them to a bed shop? They can hop about cost-free and you can have a lie-down while they're at it.

03 OPEN DAY

If you've ever fancied yourself as a fire or police officer, with a little research and planning you can bag yourself a free pass into a whole host of awesome places by taking advantage of their 'family open days'. They're normally on throughout the summer, free for the family to attend, involve kids' face-painting and usually have a burger van on site. What's not to love?

04 ROADSIDE WAVE

Instead of wasting your hard-earned cash on taking your kids to a water park, why not just introduce them to the big roadside wave next time it's raining? All you've got to do is take them somewhere that has a giant puddle at the side of the road, get them to stand on the pavement and wait until a bus goes by. Just remember to take towels!

05 PIE FEST

I know what it's like: now you're a parent you don't have the time, energy or money to attend the summer festivals, so you sit at home and pretend they don't exist. OR, you find fun family day festivals you can go to … like Pie Fest! An annual weekend festival devoted to buying, tasting and scoffing the most amazing range of pies!

06 WAX ON, WAX OFF

Want to know how to wow the kids while cleaning your car at the same time? A drive-through car wash! For some reason kids find them absolutely hysterical! For just a couple of quid you 'treat' them to an exciting adventure at the local petrol station while also giving your motor a little shine.

ARE WE THERE YET?

EVERY HOLIDAY HACK YOU'LL EVER NEED

STERILIZER ON TOUR

PACKING TO GO ON HOLIDAY can be stressful at the best of times, but when you've got the added pressure of trying to remember everything you need to keep your kid alive for a week in a foreign country, you might be heading for a nervous breakdown. Don't panic, though, as there's not much you can't just buy when you get there.

With this in mind, save yourself some space in your suitcase by not packing your entire sterilizing kit. Simply make one when you get to your holiday destination. All you need to do is buy a five-litre bottle of water from a local shop, cut the top off and drop in a couple of sterilizing tablets. EASY! Not only have you saved yourself from carting a sterilizer halfway round the world but you've also avoided having to fork out for excess baggage charges when your case tips the scales.

ROX: If you're going away with a baby under the age of one, I honestly think this is the best hack ever for sterilizing their bottles.

HOT HEAD

YOU KNOW WHAT NAPPIES ARE GREAT AT? Holding large amounts of liquid (and maybe a few solids, but that's not important for this hack). This might sound a bit mad, but if you've got a kid who's struggling with the hot weather and finding it difficult to stay cool, a (clean) nappy could be the perfect solution. All you need to do is pour some cold water into a nappy, leave it for a few seconds to absorb the liquid and then place it on your kid's head. I won't lie, this look probably isn't going to win a fashion award any time soon, but if you find yourself in a sticky situation, don't get in a hot flush, just grab a nappy and give your kid time to chill.

ROX: It really did keep the kid cool and (I can't believe I'm admitting this) I even put one on my head for a few hours when I sunburned it really badly!

BOTTLE SERVICE

THE BEST THING ABOUT GOING ON FAMILY HOLIDAYS abroad is that most decent resorts are all-inclusive, which means not only do you get a meal served up every few hours – be it breakfast, dinner or tea – but you also get access to as much free-flowing beer and wine as you can handle (which, let's face it, you're going to need when you're holidaying with kids).

Should you decide to venture outside of the resort for a day at the beach or in search of some 'normal English food', you'll hit the snag of being forced to spend money on booze as well as food. Or will you? Well, not if you plan ahead and make a few tactical trips to the resort bar for double spirits and decant them into an old water bottle before you head out. BOOM. Now you'll only need to buy mixer while you're out and no one will be any the wiser when you give yourself a crafty boozy top-up under the table.

ROX: At first I wasn't a fan of this dodgy behaviour but in the end it was kind of exciting to sneak a cheeky vodka when you shouldn't really. I'm sure it made it taste better!

LITTLE SQUIRT

WANT TO CAUSE A SPLASH ROUND THE POOL while saving yourself a bucket load on poolside toys? Easy – just reach for the medicine syringes! Whether you realize it or not, those tiny dispensers you get free with bottles of children's medicine are PERFECT miniature water pistols for your kids to drench themselves with. They're cheaper than real water pistols (that they'll probably only play with once a year) and best of all, they don't hold enough water to scare you half to death when the kids target you while you're sunning yourself on your lounger.

ROX: These are super cute and so much fun to play with. Our eldest loves them so much he used them as bath toys when we got back from the holiday.

NAPPY SAFE

WE'VE ALL BEEN THERE: you're sitting on the beach in the sun, enjoying a lukewarm overpriced beer that you've just bought from some bloke's cool bag (not a euphemism), when your kid decides they want you to take them down to the sea for a swim and a splash about. However, there's one problem: if you go pratting about in the sea, what are you going to do with your wallet and phone? Obviously you can't take them with you, but the thought of leaving them behind induces a panic attack because everyone in the world other than you is a thieving swine.

So what's the solution? A (fake) dirty nappy, of course! Drop your wallet, keys, phone, and any other valuables into a fresh nappy, seal it tight as if it contains the mother of all explosions, and tie it in a nappy bag. Chuck it on your towel in plain sight and head off to the sea, safe in the knowledge that no one in their right mind is ever going to steal what they think is a dirty nappy.

> ROX: This is bloody GENIUS! I was so worried about leaving our valuables when I was chasing the kid up and down the beach, but the minute Mark did this I totally chilled out as I knew no one would ever go near it.

BONUS TIP: *If you're looking for added plausibility, smear some melted chocolate on to the handles of the nappy bag.*

POOLSIDE PEN

IF YOU'VE NEVER HAD THE 'PLEASURE' of holidaying with a baby before, let's just say the first time is a baptism of fire. Long gone are the holidays where you chill by the pool with a rum and pineapple, listening to music. Now, your days consist of smothering your child in SPF 50 every ten minutes, worrying how long their milk can stay out of the fridge and desperately trying to find shady places to keep them cool.

However, there is still hope of some relaxation *if* you've remembered to pack one key inflatable: a paddling pool. It sounds mental to pack a paddling pool for a week in a hotel but, believe me, it's worth its weight in gold. Simply fill it with about an inch of water, place it under a sun umbrella next to your poolside lounger and BOOM … you've just made the perfect mini playpen for your baby. It will not only keep them cool but will also stop them crawling off and face planting into the swimming pool. Now, where's that hotel waiter with my cocktail?!

ROX: I loved this for sitting around the pool and so did lots of other families who kept asking us where we got it from. Can't recommend it enough.

AIRTIGHT APPS

NONE OF US LIKE TO ADMIT IT in front of other judgy parents but, let's face it, the smartphone is the greatest thing ever to happen to parenthood. Don't get me wrong, I wouldn't recommend you let your kid sit and play on it for thirteen hours straight, but if you're attempting to watch the second half of the footy, desperately trying to scoff the rest of your meal, or even just wanting to jump in the shower for the first time in three days … it's perfect.

However, daring to catch a few rays on the beach in peace while letting your kid smash through your monthly data allowance by watching toy reviews on YouTube is quite likely to result in your phone ending up socket-down in the sand or, worse still, being lobbed into the sea. So, to avoid an insurance claim, make sure you take a sandwich bag to the beach with you, pop your phone in it, seal it shut and you're good to go! Now you've just got to find something to put your sandwiches in. 😊

ROX: Mark does tend to pack some 'unusual' things when we go away but never did I expect a sandwich bag to become a beach phone case!

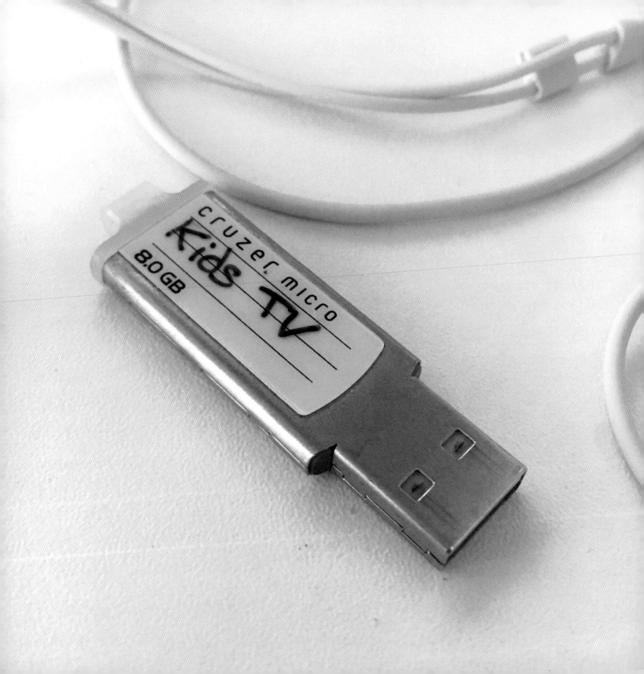

TAKEAWAY TV

DO YOU WANT TO KNOW HOW YOUR KID can watch their favourite TV shows even when you're on holiday? Take the programmes with you! Instead of having to race through the channels on your hotel TV, trying to find a re-run of Mr Tumble before eventually settling for an aggressive-sounding Spanish cartoon, you can instead make a sick USB compilation of all your kid's favourite shows before you leave! All you need to do is download a few of their fave shows online, load them on to a USB stick, then plug it into the telly when you get there. Pretty much every hotel room on the planet now has a flat-screen telly, so I guarantee you won't struggle to find a USB socket.

ROX: It's not until you're away from so many home comforts that you realize how impressive this idea really is. It's helped to chill and calm our boy on more than one holiday.

BONUS TIP: Remember to pack your kid some headphones so you don't have to listen to it.

BEACH-BED-SUN-LOUNGER-LILO

WHOEVER INVENTED THE CONCEPT of renting sun loungers on the beach is both a genius … and a massive penis. They're basically charging you for a place to lie down which is 5 inches higher than where you can lie down for free. It's mental! So here's an epic hack to save you some cash: take your own blow-up mattress down to the beach with you. A single size is exactly the same dimensions as a lounger, it can be inflated in a matter of minutes, it's more comfortable because it moulds to fit the shape of your body so not only is this hack saving you €10 a day, it's keeping you comfy too. Come on, tell me that isn't amazing!

ROX: Watching Mark with an air bed and a foot pump on a beach in 24-degree heat made me laugh so much. I still can't believe he packed a blow-up bed to go on holiday but he swears it's a holiday 'game-changer'.

POPPING BOTTLES

I CAN'T TAKE FULL CREDIT for inventing this hack, but since I don't think Laura from the all-inclusive snack bar in Benidorm is going to be releasing a parenting hacks book any time soon, I'm pretty sure she won't mind me borrowing it. It's probably one of the simplest and most effective ideas you'll find anywhere. With nothing more than a straw and a sharp object (penknife/car key/corkscrew) you can turn a regular bottle of water into a child-friendly drinking fountain. Just make a small hole in the cap by poking your sharp object into it, and then feed the straw through the hole … THAT'S IT! You now have a sealed drinking bottle and the water can either be sucked through the straw or squirted into your kid's mouth to avoid any spillages if they've not yet mastered how to use a cup.

ROX: One word: brilliant! A child doesn't even need to know how to use a straw as the water can just be squeezed into their mouth. It took the hassle out of having to re-fill a sippy cup, and this way you know the water is always fresh.

SIX TIPS FOR TRAVELLING WITH A BABY

HERE'S THE DEFINITIVE LIST of LadBaby's top tips for holidaying with a baby. Believe me, nothing hits first-time parents harder than the thought of getting their bottles of breastmilk through airport security, worrying if your kid can cope with the 'extremities' of foreign weather, or wondering whether your hotel will have adequate sleeping arrangements. So here are a few tips to ease your woes.

01 PACKING

New parents have a tendency to pack their kid's entire wardrobe when they go away. On our first trip abroad, there could have been an alien invasion, a zombie apocalypse or a full-blown *Waterworld*-style flood and we'd have had an outfit for it. I'm not saying don't prepare, but nobody wants to see a baby dressed like Kevin Costner … do they?

02 THE PLANE

Don't panic about it. Obviously it will be hard work and the baby will probably cry at the worst possible time, but just get on with it. Inevitably there will always be someone on the plane who's got a problem with kids, but honestly, who cares? If they didn't want to travel with families they should have chartered their own private jet.

03 THE STROLLER

Whether you're buying a 'holiday buggy' or simply taking your normal one away with you, make sure it has a reclining function (or turns into a bed!). When you're at a bar, sipping ice-cold San Miguels and eating handfuls of peanuts, having a buggy that turns into a mini bed on wheels for your napping kid is the greatest thing on the planet.

04 SLEEPING

To help your baby nod off without complaint in a foreign land, take some of their bedding essentials from home. It might sound mad but adding the comfort of a familiar sheet and favourite teddy is the difference between being able to enjoy an evening sangria on the balcony and spending all night soothing a restless tot in a travel cot.

05 NAPPY CHANGING

Nappy-changing facilities in toilets abroad aren't always a given. Other than at the airport and the hotel, nappy-changing will mainly take place on benches, table tops or just closed toilet seats. My advice is to make sure that you've always got the changing mat and nappy bags to hand as you never know where the next change might have to take place.

06 FAN

If you use no other tip from this list, then please use this one: buy a battery-powered clippable fan! Whether it's fastened to the buggy, the cot, the plane seat or the dinner table, it'll be the best money you'll ever spend. I'm sure you can get them from anywhere but, again, it'll be easier to find one before you leave.

CLOCKING OFF

THE AFTER-HOURS PARENT HACKS
YOU NEVER KNEW YOU NEEDED

BEER-BY CARRIER

SO HERE'S A PROBLEM EVERY PARENT on the planet will face at some point or other. What on earth are you going to do with the hoards of baby kit once the kids have grown out of it? It's pointless to keep it all unless you're having another child or you're going to start mothering the dog and dressing it up in the kids' old clothes. Do you bin it? Do you try to palm it off on someone at a car-boot sale and run the risk of only getting a tenner for something you spent over a hundred quid on? Instead, why not just find a new use for everything?

Take the baby carrier, for example: that can easily be converted into a shopping carrier. If you've got to bring something really heavy home, like, say … a crate of beer, just pop the baby carrier on and strap it to your chest. It's far more convenient than putting it in a bag, as you'll still have both your arms free. PLUS, you avoid the 5p bag charge! It all adds up.

ROX: I can't wait to use the carrier at a festival one day. I'll be the girl in sequins carrying a box of wine as though it's a baby!

COFFEE COASTERS

IF YOU ASK ANY PARENT what they want more than anything during the first few weeks after having a baby, I guarantee they'll say 'a nanny, a live-in chef, a full-time cleaner and a professional masseuse'. But after that they'll say 'COFFEE'. Lots and lots of coffee. And if you're breastfeeding you'll probably have access to an endless supply of disposable coasters, i.e. breast pads. Yep, you might not realize it but breast pads are the perfect size and shape to put your cuppa down on and are designed to soak up excess drippage. So next time your other half is sitting down to start feeding, or expressing, and you're searching for something to put your mug on, look no further than inside your partner's bra … Just make sure you ask first. 😊

ROX: Sleep deprivation makes me super clumsy so this was ideal for me when I was breastfeeding!

NACHO FLAP

UNLESS YOU'RE A PROFESSIONAL BODY BUILDER, champion axe thrower or world-renowned arm wrestler, the chances are you're probably not going to be prepared for the demands that parenthood is going to place on your upper body. From the minute your child arrives you'll basically have to relearn how to do everything with just one hand, as your new prince or princess will need to be carried EVERYWHERE you go!

The advantage is that within a few short weeks one of your arms will be strong enough to go fifteen rounds with Rocky Balboa. The disadvantage is that your other arm will be solely responsible for keeping you clothed and fed … which is harder than it sounds. If you don't believe me, try putting on (and tying) your shoes with one hand!

Anyway, make life easier for yourself by nicking the hard plastic flap window from the top of an empty packet of wet wipes and attaching it to the front or back of an unopened bag of crisps. The easy-access system can be easily navigated with one hand and means that even if you end up going shopping in bare feet, you'll at least be well fed.

ROX: Why the hell aren't crisp packets already made like this? Just saying!

208

THE MEGA-STRAW-ROUS

YOU KNOW THE PHRASE 'never wake a sleeping baby'? Unfortunately, that applies even when your kid's decided to have a kip in your arms. You can risk it for a biscuit and chance moving them, putting them down or shifting your weight to free up an arm … but I can guarantee the moment you shuffle even an inch you'll regret it. Thanks to this nifty hack, though, you can at least stay hydrated by making your own giant straw in advance so your drink is always within reach.

Grab two, three, four, or even five free straws from the bar and simply shove them all together to make one long Mega-straw-rous. There might be a bit of collateral damage with each suck – there's bound to be a bit of liquid loss – but believe me, it's better than not having a drink at all for the duration of the baby's nap.

ROX: This photo always makes me smile. FYI this works beautifully with a glass of wine, too, and is totally classy.

BASKET CASE

IN A RUSH BUT NEED TO POP TO THE SHOPS to pick something up? Maybe you're off to a party but you've forgotten to buy a present for little Johnny's second birthday? Well, thanks to the humble shopping basket you can do your emergency shop at speed without having to chase your kid around the aisles as they get distracted by everything in sight. Simply pop your child in the basket and off you go. If they start getting bored, feel free to drop a little toy in with them to keep them entertained. Then, as long as you don't mess about, it should keep them quiet just long enough for you to go and get little Johnny a massive drum kit, or something equally as annoying to terrorize his parents with.

ROX: I have so many photos of Mark doing this with our eldest when he was little. He always loved it and they'd follow me round shops, laughing and playing.

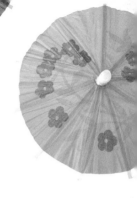

FRUIT POUCH COCKTAILS

IT'S A PARENTING CLICHÉ but I don't care … I hate throwing away food. Whether it's been left on someone's plate or in the fridge, if food destined for the bin can be salvaged, then why not! It poses a bit of a problem, though, when your baby has only just started on solid food and is eating purées. Have you got the stomach to wolf down half-finished jars and pouches of mushy baby food? I think it's more of a psychological than a physical hurdle to overcome, but the texture alone can be enough to set off even the strongest of gag reflexes.

So, is there anything that can be done? Well, as a lot of baby food is fruit-based, why not turn the leftover purée into a cocktail? It might sound weird but if you dilute some fruity mush with a double vodka and a few ice cubes you'll be amazed at the results. Give it a shot – or two!

ROX: Never one to turn down a cocktail, this little trick worked so well I could never tell the difference between a shop-bought tipple and one that Mark had made.

BABY FACE

YOU MIGHT BE WELL PAST YOUR TEENAGE YEARS but unfortunately that doesn't necessarily mean you're immune to enormous spots appearing on your face without a second's warning. Whether one's popped up overnight to encompass your entire snout or has been developing gradually over a number of weeks, having a massive spot surface on your face is annoying at any age. So now you're wondering why a spot remedy is cropping up in a parenting book. The answer: Sudocrem! Not only is this magical cream perfect for sorting out a chapped arse – it's also 'spot on' for sorting out your face. Just rub a generous dollop on your troublesome zit before heading to bed and I promise it'll look better by the morning.

ROX: I started doing this when I ran out of tea-tree oil spot cream and found it worked better for me than so many expensive products I'd used in the past. Although I did end up buying my own pot so I didn't have to worry about cross-contamination and potentially getting poo on my face.

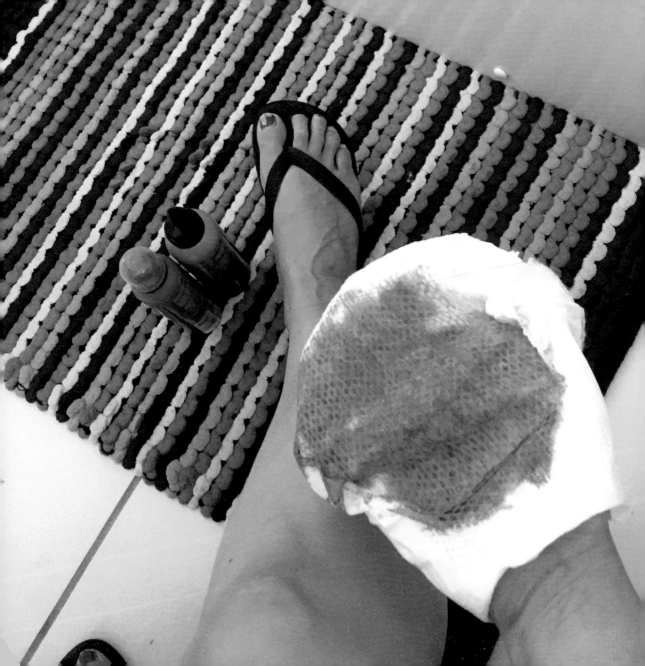

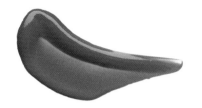

TANNING NAPPY

HERE'S THE PERFECT PRE-/POST-SUMMER HACK to make sure every mum (or dad) has that special glow about them all year round. With nothing more than a (clean) nappy you can make yourself the cheapest and easiest tanning mitt the world has ever seen. All you need to do is turn the nappy inside out, slip your hand in it and then fasten it using the little tabs on either side before using it to apply your fake tan. Personally, oranging up to look like an Oompa-Loompa has never really been high on my list of life goals … but each to their own, I guess.

Just a heads-up, remember to throw the nappy away once you're done. The last thing you want to be doing is trying to explain why your kid's got an orange arse at the next weigh-in!

ROX: This is such a good alternative to a shop-bought hand mitt if you don't already have one.

HOT SHOT COFFEE

IF THERE'S ONE PIECE OF MODERN-DAY BABY KIT every new family has it's the Tommee Tippee Perfect Prep. If you're new to parenting (or have been living in a cave for the last few years), you might not know this, but it's basically a godsend of a machine that can deliver room-temperature water to make up formula within a matter of minutes, time after time. Grandparents hate it because they think that 'parents of today have it too easy' but it means that when your baby's up at 2 a.m., screaming the house down for a feed, you're not desperately trying to cool down some freshly boiled water.

A little-known fact about this gadget is that it can also be unofficially converted into an espresso machine. All you've got to do is turn the dial up to 11, place an espresso cup containing some instant coffee under the spout and then hit start! The machine will pump out enough boiling-hot water for the perfect single espresso. (Don't press the button again, though – you don't want it topped up with the cold stuff!) If you're getting up at 5 a.m. with the kid, at least you'll be wide awake!

ROX: LIFE-SAVER. Caffeine-hits galore!
I probably made more cups of coffee
with this than I did bottles of milk.

BBQ SAFETY GRILL

The best thing about summer (other than drinking beer outside whenever the temperature hits double figures) is that it's the only time of year you can legitimately get home from work, pour lighter fluid on an open fire and eat burnt chicken legs half-naked in your garden without your neighbours kicking off. Sure, there's the possibility you might get food poisoning and that you might set Janice-next-door's fence on fire, but still, nothing tastes better than a chargrilled quarter-pounder!

The only problem is … how do you parent and barbecue at the same time without anything or anyone getting burnt? The solution: dig out the old baby playpen from the garage! It's the ultimate device for keeping the BBQ away from inquisitive little hands while still offering you easy access for flipping the burgers and turning the sausages. BOOM! Now you've just got to hope you remembered to pick up the burger buns.

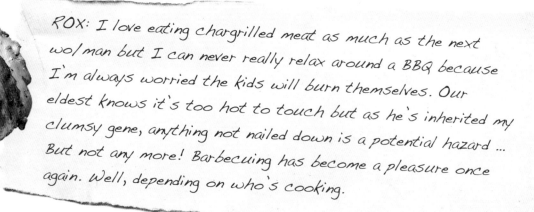

ROX: I love eating chargrilled meat as much as the next wo/man but I can never really relax around a BBQ because I'm always worried the kids will burn themselves. Our eldest knows it's too hot to touch but as he's inherited my clumsy gene, anything not nailed down is a potential hazard … But not any more! Barbecuing has become a pleasure once again. Well, depending on who's cooking.

BONUS TIP: *Crack out the playpen again at Christmas and use it to protect your tree from the kids … and the pets.*

THAT'S A WRAP

Thanks to everyone who's bought and read *Parenting for £1*, and to all the incredible people who have supported LadBaby and helped to make this book a reality. I sincerely hope we've helped you to dip, dodge and duck some of parenting's biggest expenses and have put a smile on your face during every nappy change and following every sleepless night.

Introducing a baby to this world (and to your bank manager) is one of the most financially crippling decisions you'll ever make, so do whatever you can to save yourself a few quid and keep your family happy. If you've got an epic dad hack, money-saving masterstroke or game-changing top tip that you think I've missed, do post it online using the hashtag #ParentingForAPound and I'll share all the best ideas on LadBaby.

As for me, wish me luck as I continue my online journey into responsible parenting. And don't forgot to give my book a cracking review on Amazon so I can impress my publisher and convince them to let me write *Teenaging for £1* in a few years. Yes maaaaaate!!!

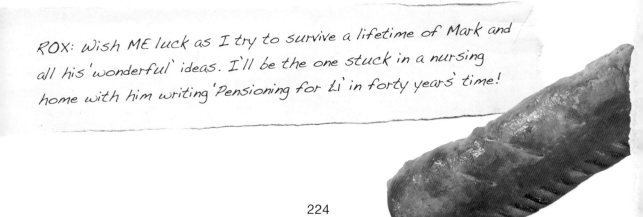

ROX: Wish ME luck as I try to survive a lifetime of Mark and all his 'wonderful' ideas. I'll be the one stuck in a nursing home with him writing 'Pensioning for £1' in forty years' time!